AF559295

Older Ways

Traditional Nova Scotian Craftsmen

Older Ways

Traditional Nova Scotian Craftsmen

Peter Barss

Craft Notes by Joleen Gordon

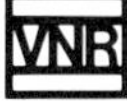

Van Nostrand Reinhold Ltd., Toronto,
New York, Cincinnati, London, Melbourne

Library of Congress Catalogue Number 80-52728

Canadian Cataloguing in Publication Data
Barss, Peter, 1941-
Older ways

ISBN 0-442-29628-2

1. Art industries and trade—Nova Scotia.
2. Artisans—Nova Scotia. I. Gordon, Joleen.
II. Title.

NK842.N6B57 745'.0971 C80-094625-1

This book would not have been possible without the generous support of:
Art Gallery of Mount Saint Vincent University
Nova Scotia Museum
Nova Scotia Department of Culture, Recreation and Fitness
Explorations Programme of The Canada Council
National Museums Programme

All photographs are by Peter Barss
Text recorded and edited by Peter Barss
Transcription by Joleen Gordon and Myra Barss
Editorial consultant: James T. Wills
Design: Hugh Michaelson
Illustrations: Taiya Barss
Typesetting: Alpha Graphics Limited
Printing and binding: The Bryant Press

Printed and bound in Canada

80 81 82 83 84 85 86 7 6 5 4 3 2 1

For the men and women represented
in *Older Ways* who so generously shared part
of their lives with us.

Contents

Foreword

Nova Scotia is bulging with craftsmen. Every second week there seems to be a craft show somewhere, and craft shops have appeared on every street corner.

But the craftsmen of today and those of yesterday are, for the most part, two different species. The craftsmen of today have an urge to create, an urge to satisfy their inner feelings. They hope that their work will appeal to the eye of the customer as something interesting, unique or artistic. The craftsmen of yesterday, at least those chosen by Peter and Joleen, were of a different sort. Their products were designed to fill a need; they created necessities required by their neighbours in their daily lives.

We shouldn't think for a minute that because these people were making practical, useful objects, they were any less creative, artistic, sensitive or knowledgeable than today's craftsmen. They were, in many cases, masters of their craft, highly creative and extremely sensitive to the basic needs of their fellow man. It is also rather alarming to me that despite our advances in education in recent years these people knew many things that we are no longer taught.

If a craftsman today wants to build a wheel, he goes to the lumberyard, buys some stock and hopes for the best. Yesterday, he selected his species of wood carefully for the purpose —oak for the spokes, beech for the felloes, yellow birch for the hubs. He cut his trees late in the fall when the moisture content was lowest. He didn't limb them immediately but allowed them to lie in their limbs to draw out even more moisture. After sawing the logs into various dimensions for his purposes, he dried them slowly and carefully, one year to the inch of thickness. He shaped his wheel with loving care and with a knowledge of his craft passed down to him by many generations of skilled craftsmen.

Some of these people still live. Today they are as unique as their crafts. Peter and Joleen searched them out, talked to them and portray them here in a way that makes us realize clearly that not only the craftsmen are unique.

I have a deep admiration for Peter and Joleen. Their work in assembling this book clearly demonstrates their artistry, but even more importantly, it demonstrates their sensitivity, their deep understanding and their love for those people who have much to teach us about the older ways.

J.L. Martin, Director
Nova Scotia Museum

Preface

Not so many years ago, the relative isolation of communities in Nova Scotia demanded that they be nearly self-sufficient. In a very basic way, the survival of a community depended on the resourcefulness of the individuals who lived in it; each member of the community had a contribution to make. Farms were worked by oxen, which meant that somebody in the village had to know how to chip out a yoke and fit it to the team. A wheelwright would fashion the wheels for the wagon and plow, someone else a whip. And the local blacksmith would shoe the oxen. The men and women who acquired these skills were "ordinary people." Their crafts evolved out of the necessities of everyday life.

Archie McKnight is a blacksmith. He has worked hard all his life and, at seventy-seven, still does. He can tell us how to soften a piece of iron and shape it into a pair of ox shoes, how its colour in the fire indicates the precise moment it should be struck on the anvil, what kind of hammer to use and how to use it. He knows the farmers and their teams of oxen; he will meet their particular requirements. And Archie has his own standards of workmanship. Each pair of ox shoes he makes bears the stamp of his character. There is no remote technology here. A bond exists between Archie, the objects he makes and their ultimate function; his work links him to his community and to his fellow man.

Archie doesn't shoe many oxen now. The tractors that have taken their place signal a new way of life – one that often slights the community of man. "Somethin' I often think about . . . the people today, they don't have time to stop an' talk to you. Now in them days, you had a

horse an' wagon. An' when you drove by, why if you was anywheres near a feller, you'd stop an' talk to him. The people aren't as happy an' contented today. . . always lookin' for somethin' they can't get, it seems to me."
Archie has left his horse and wagon behind, but he has not forgotten the importance of stopping "to talk to a feller."

Listen to Archie McKnight and listen to the other people represented in *Older Ways*. Their values, like their crafts, grew out of a spirit of community.

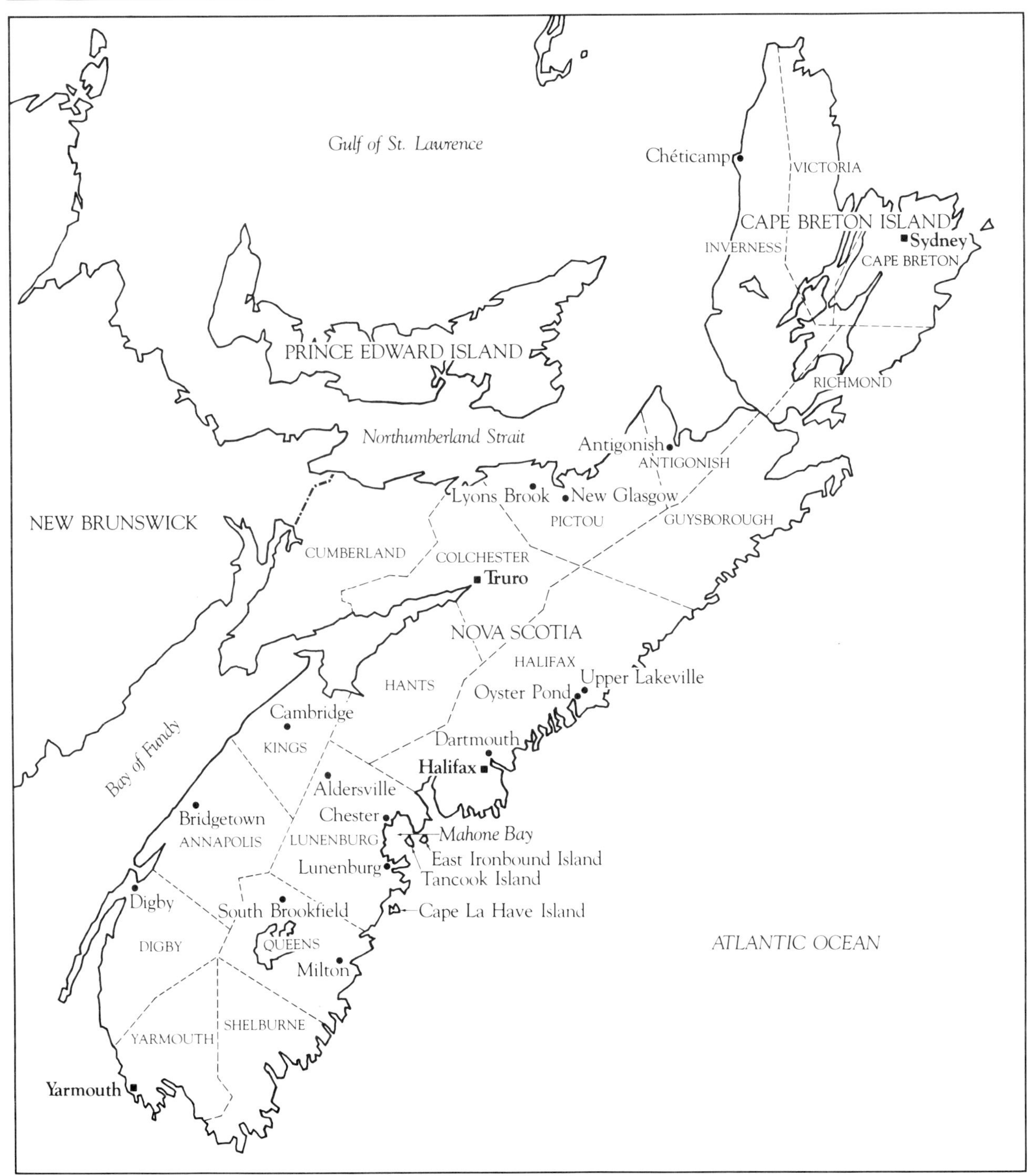

Gulf of St. Lawrence
Chéticamp
VICTORIA
CAPE BRETON ISLAND
Sydney
INVERNESS
CAPE BRETON
PRINCE EDWARD ISLAND
RICHMOND
Northumberland Strait
Antigonish
ANTIGONISH
Lyons Brook
New Glasgow
NEW BRUNSWICK
PICTOU
GUYSBOROUGH
CUMBERLAND
COLCHESTER
Truro
NOVA SCOTIA
HALIFAX
Upper Lakeville
HANTS
Oyster Pond
Cambridge
Bay of Fundy
Dartmouth
KINGS
Halifax
Aldersville
Bridgetown
Chester
ANNAPOLIS
LUNENBURG
Mahone Bay
East Ironbound Island
Lunenburg
Tancook Island
Digby
South Brookfield
Cape La Have Island
DIGBY
QUEENS
ATLANTIC OCEAN
Milton
SHELBURNE
YARMOUTH
Yarmouth

Older Ways

Traditional Nova Scotian Craftsmen

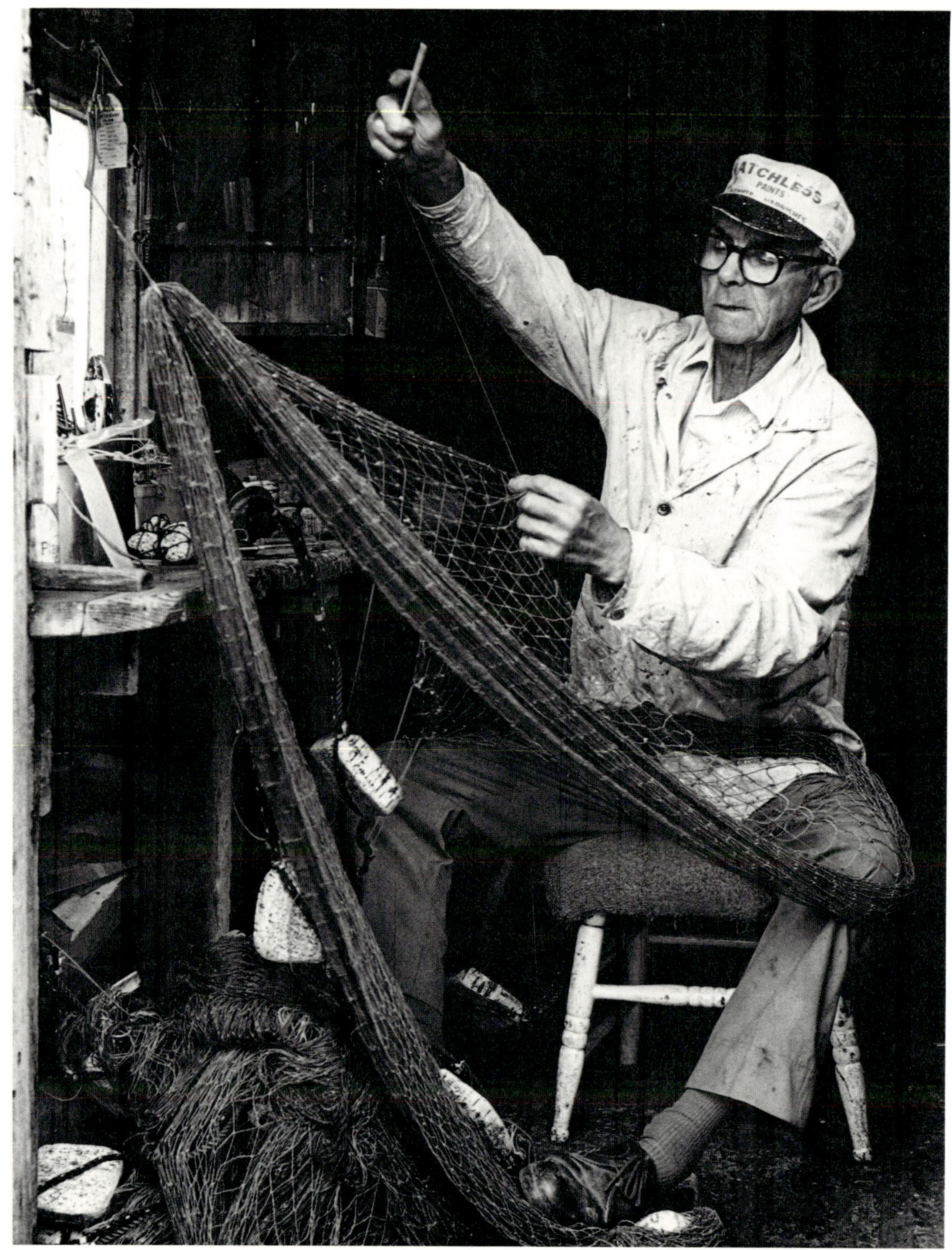

Carl Bush

Born 25 February 1906, Fish Nets

Well, when I learnt to knit nets, it was years ago. I was only ten years old. My uncle, Steve Bush, an old gentleman in West Dublin, he taught me how to make 'em. He used to go out to Cape LaHave to be nearer to the fishin' waters. He had a shanty out there. We used to go out an' stay there for a whole week. I was with 'im – help 'im out. See, I used to go with 'im in the boat . . . go out to the nets an' help 'im pick herring out o' the nets. He learnt me to knit nets. An' in the evenin's, we'd mend the nets that was tore.

Now in the wintertime, them old fellers, they'd knit nets. I've spent a good many nights – all night, right here. I worked all day, knit all night – go to work the next day an' sleep that night. 'Course now no one makes his own nets – they're all nylon now, made onto machines. I mend 'em, mind you – mend 'em an' rig 'em – but the full net, the twine is store-bought nowadays.

One night I was out here last winter, this winter gone . . . an' I was mending an' at three o'clock I fell asleep. An' when I woke up, I had my needle in my hand an' my other hand had a'hold the net. Sittin' right in this chair right in the middle of the floor here, like that. I had the needle in my hand where I had it fast to the net. It was five-thirty when I woke up. Two hours an' a half I slept right here. I was so tired.

Yes sir, I've rigged a good many nets. If they ain't rigged right, they won't fish right. See, the mesh has got to hang right for different fish – one way for herring an' a little fuller for mackerel. Then in the spring, the mesh is smaller 'cause the fish that is runnin' is thinner than the fall fish. You got to take a lot into account. Now I rigged ten nets for Dawson

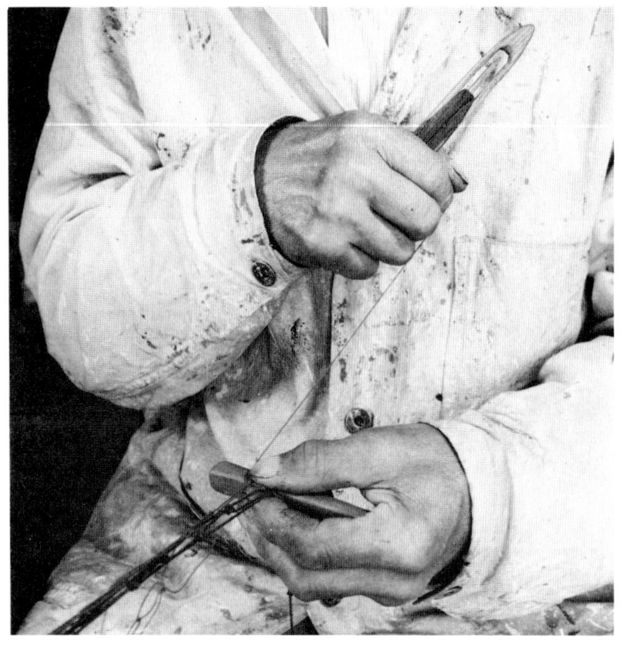

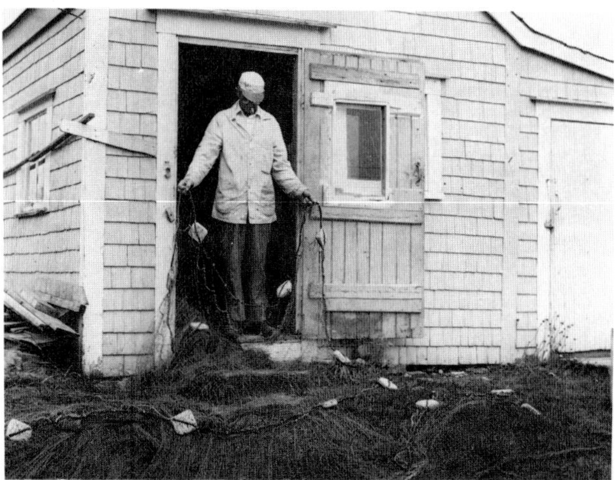

Baker – he told me how he wanted 'em, an' I rigged 'em that way. "Why," he says, "you certainly done some job on my nets. I'm proud of 'em," he said. "The way they're hung – if them don't fish, nothin' will." There's lots o' fellers around that can't do it – can't sit down an' rig nets or mend nets like I do.

Today, fishermen can buy machine-made synthetic yarn nets in a variety of mesh sizes to be rigged according to fishing conditions. Before the invention of synthetic yarns and knitting machines, the men bought imported cotton twine and "knit" their own nets using hand-carved needles and net gauges. Boys learned to make nets in their pre-teens. At first glance, the netting does not appear to resemble the more common form of knitting found in sweaters and mittens, but closer examination shows that the "fabric" is produced by inserting one loop through another, which is the definition of "knitting."

In the photograph, Carl Bush is holding a herring net. Once the net is knit, it is rigged with buoys, weights and is hung on a headrope. The buoys or "corks" are made out of big wooden jug corks: "They'd saw 'em out into blocks, an' then make 'em to whatever shape they wanted... take their knife an' cut the ridges into 'em for to put the headrope in. Then, a lot of them got the idea to cut their initials onto their buoys and to paint 'em. My colours are white and red." Carl makes three kinds of buoys for his nets: "... the standin' buoy would be on the mooring... when the weight of the net comes, that would pull on it an' straighten it right up." When one end is moored and the other swings free, a "play buoy" is attached to the free end; "that buoy would swing right round, end to end...." The "bobber buoys" are fixed at certain intervals along the length of the headrope to hold the net up in the water.

Traditionally, the net is weighted with "sinker rocks" tied to the bottom line of the net, generally one below each cork, but this arrangement differs depending on how the net is to be fished and on the fishing experience of the net-maker. These sinker rocks are small bags knit of cotton twine, each containing a small round beach stone. They are not made too heavy, but of a weight sufficient to open up the meshwork so the net can catch fish.

"Hanging a net" refers to how much the meshwork is gathered before it is attached to the headrope. In a "full" net the meshwork is not gathered as much as it is in a "not so full" net, which means the mesh stretches open easily and the net is more efficient in catching fatter fish like mackerel as opposed to the thinner herring.

In the days before powered boats, fishermen would have five, six or perhaps ten at the most of these hand-made nets. Nowadays, an inshore fisherman might own as many as thirty to forty. Some inshore fishermen still use cotton nets, which must be tanned to preserve the twine and keep it from rotting. The old way of tanning with tree bark is still used. Certain barks, such as hemlock and alder, have a strong brown dye which is released in boiling water. These barks are used on their own or in combination with "cutch," an imported substance prepared from the wood of the *Acaia Catechu* tree found in India, Burma and Borneo. The dark brown cutch is dissolved in the boiling water heated in large iron tanpots. Some fishermen tan their nets in this way twice each year.

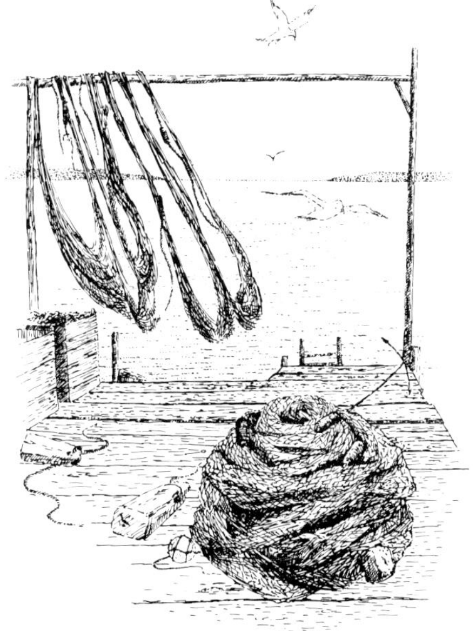

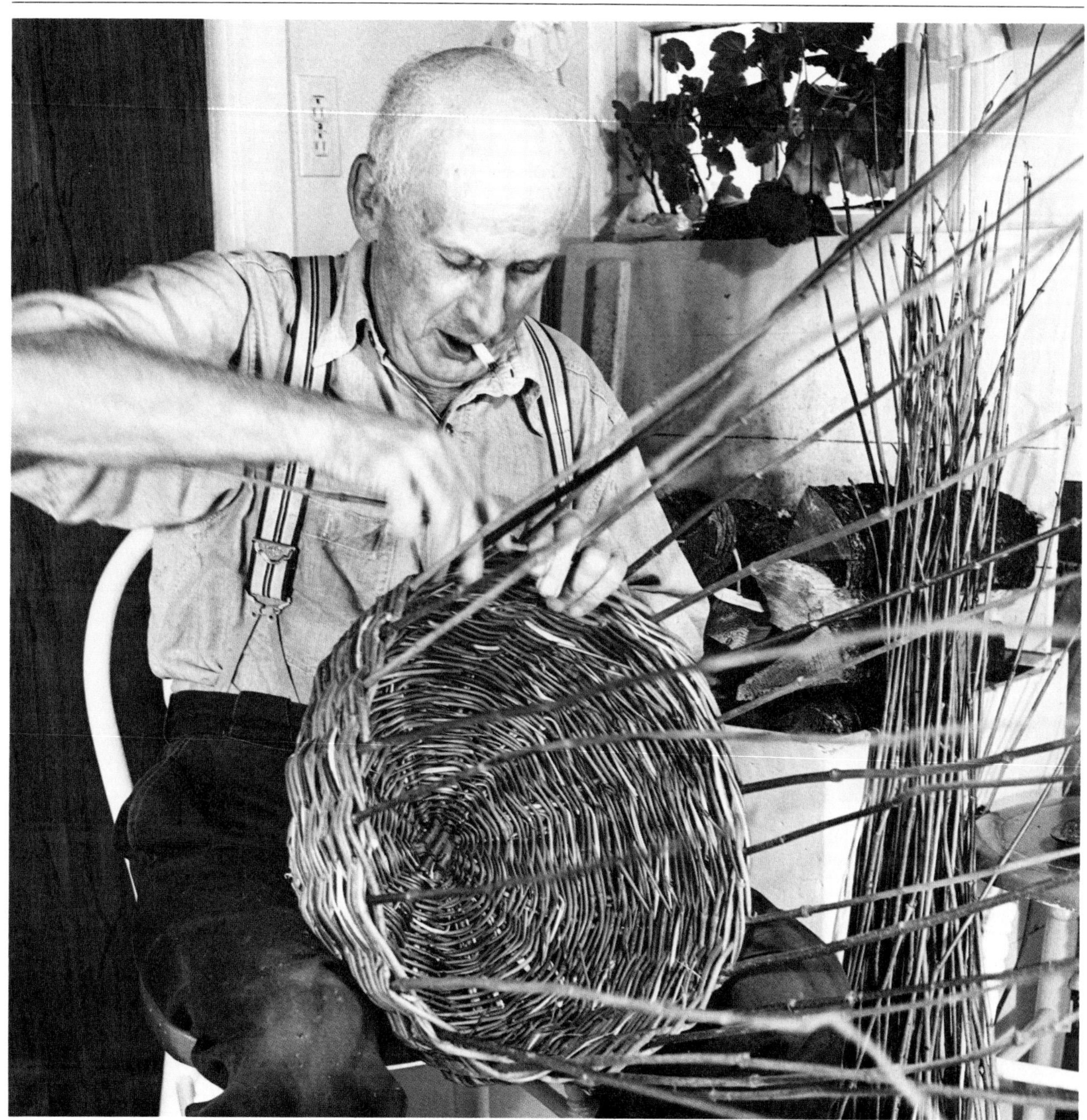

Bernard Mossman

Born 17 February 1907, Witherod Baskets

The old people, they all had these baskets. The old fellers back then, well, like my father an' those before him, they all made 'em for their own use. They all could make 'em. They were German people who came here, and they were the first ones who started it . . . my grandfather, he was of German descent. I picked it up by takin' it over from my father. I wanted my daddy to show me, an' he gave me an old one that was layin' around an' he says, "Take that apart, boy, an' you'll soon find out how to make one." I was only young then, maybe eight or ten. Well I did take it apart. That's how I picked up how to make 'em – from then on I knowed how.

I'd make some up when I had the time – mostly for our own use, an' sometimes sell some. You didn't get a lot o' money for 'em, but there was no trouble gettin' rid of 'em – then there was people doin' some farmin' yet, doin' a little plantin', raisin' vegetables. They used 'em for pickin' up potatoes an' stuff like that in the fields. An' when there was salt fishin' vessels goin' off to The Banks, why they'd have eight or ten of these baskets aboard of 'em for the codfish livers an' like that.

I use 'em yet – in the fall, carryin' potatoes, puttin' turnips down, carrots, all that stuff . . . settin' wood in. Why should I go an' buy a basket or a tub or somethin' when I can go in the woods an' cut the wit's an' put one together in an evenin'? I think it's just for the fun out of sayin' that I can make 'em!

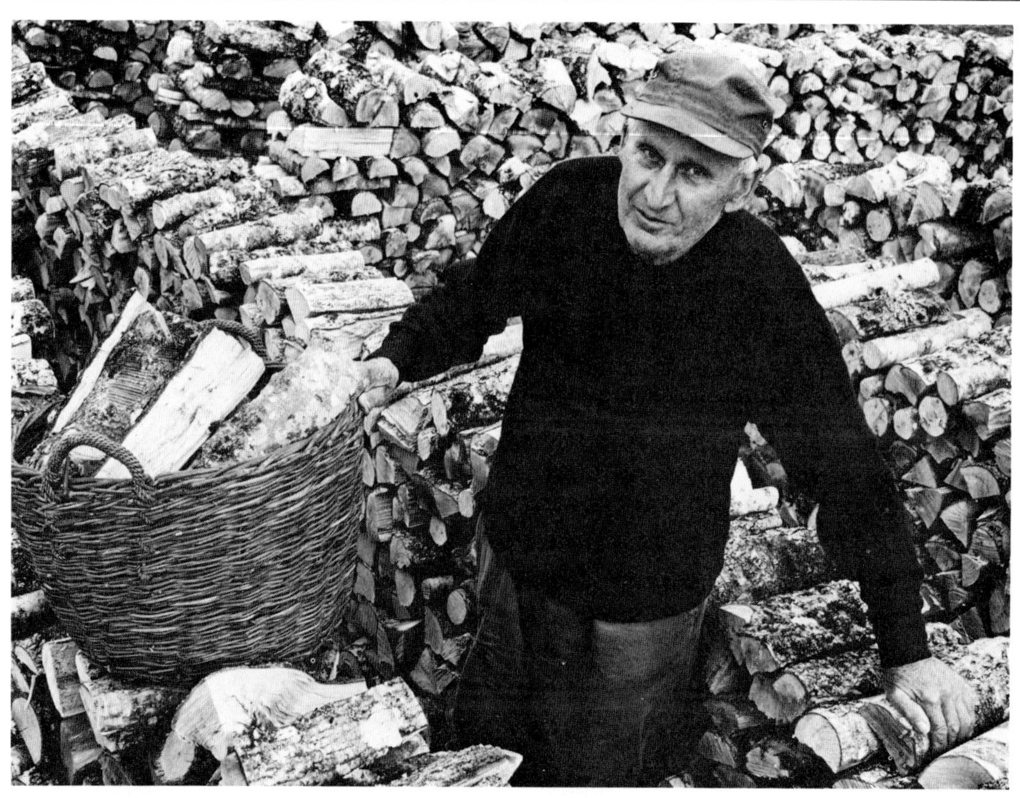

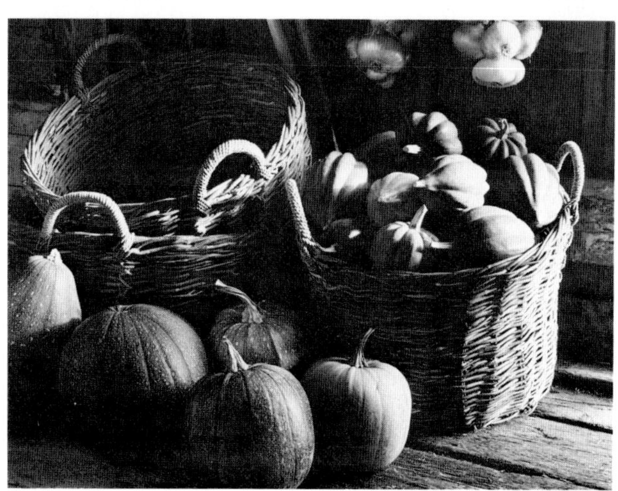

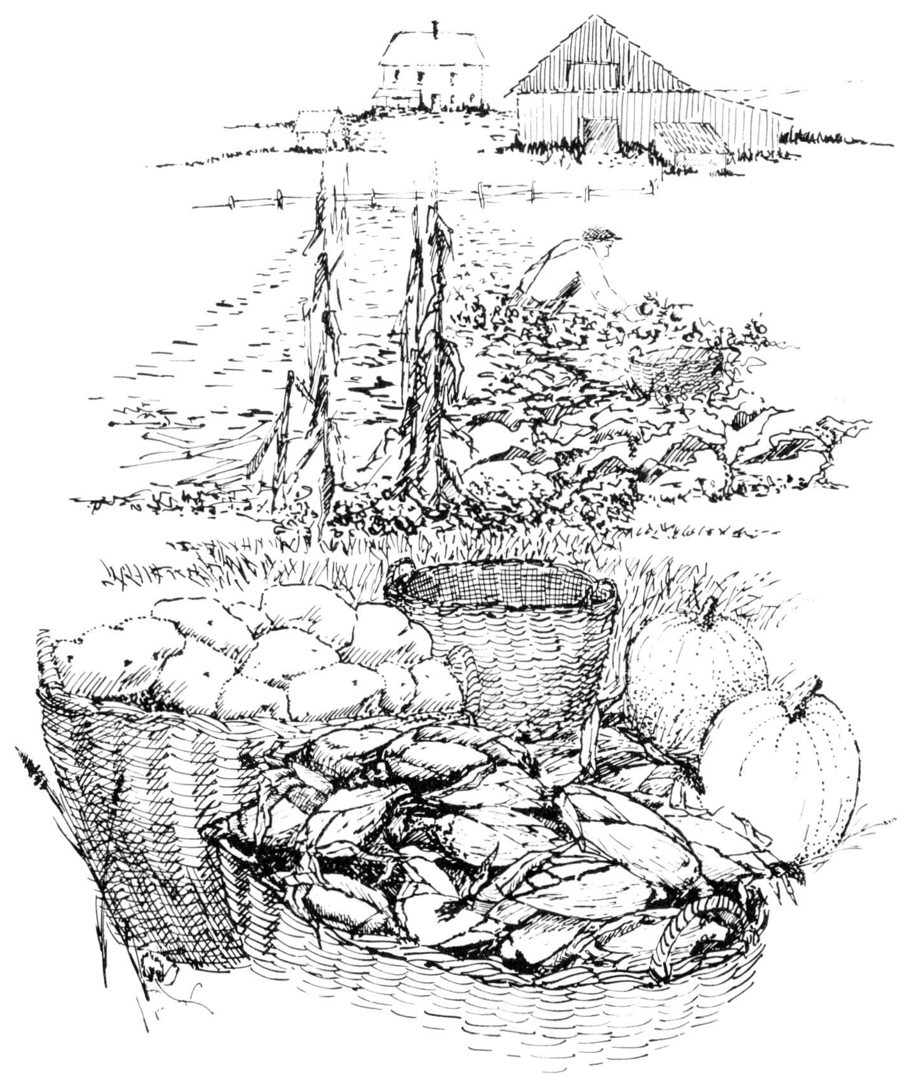

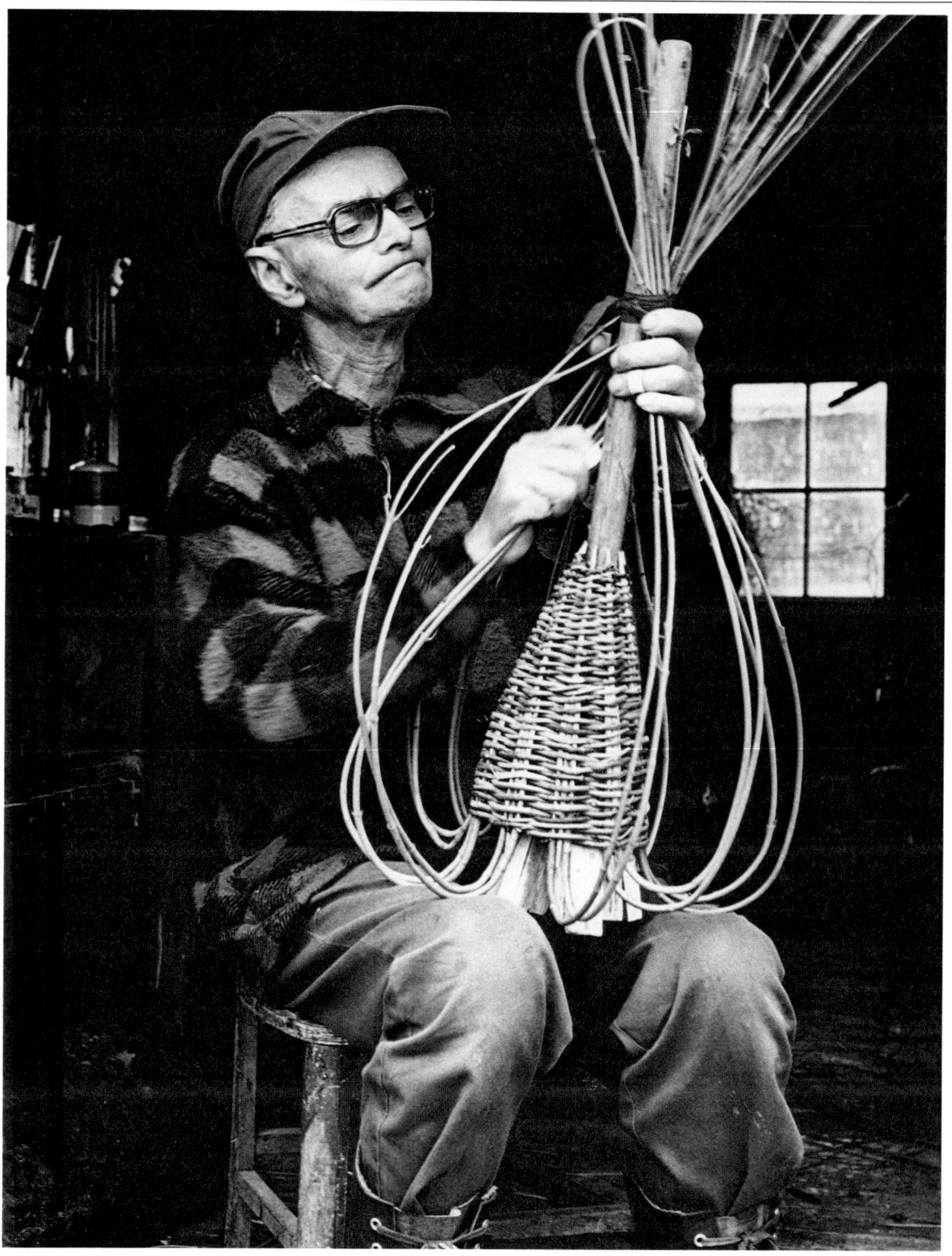

Victor Bush

Born 2 May 1902, Witherod Eelpots

I used to watch an old feller by the name o' Solly Sperry – he's dead now. But years ago he used to be out to Cape LaHave – he used to go fishin' out there in the summertime in a small boat. An' he used to sit an' make eelpots, when the weather was dirty an' he couldn't go out fishin' you know. Sit there an' make eelpots. I was only young – nine, ten year old . . . an' I used to watch him makin' these things. I said, "By golly, I'm goin' to make one o' them yet." After I seen it once I could do it. That's just where I got it from.

An' as far as wit's goes, I can put anythin' together with wit's – pretty near I guess – that you could really want. You name it, tell me the shape of it an' I'll make it. Learnt just practically all of it on my own. I learnt it, that's it. You know, stuff that you make . . . you can see it. See what you got to have – when you look at it. I can see it, before I go to work at it. That's right! Look right through it . . . see right through it. It just comes to me like that.

I say you can do a lot if you try. I worked just about all my life with my hands. Carpentry work, mendin' nets – stuff like that. It gives me a lot o' satisfactions. Really it does. An' well with these eelpots an' things . . . just do it for the stormy days for the enjoyment of it. Breaks the time up. Things . . . things go easier.

'Course today people got a lot o' machinery to do work. Years ago, everythin' was done by hand. Let the fellers do that today! You got to put it on the machine. Zoom – that's it . . . but it's not the same. You do it quicker on a machine – that's the part of it. You got to have it all done quick. Quicker you got it done the better . . . but it's not the same.

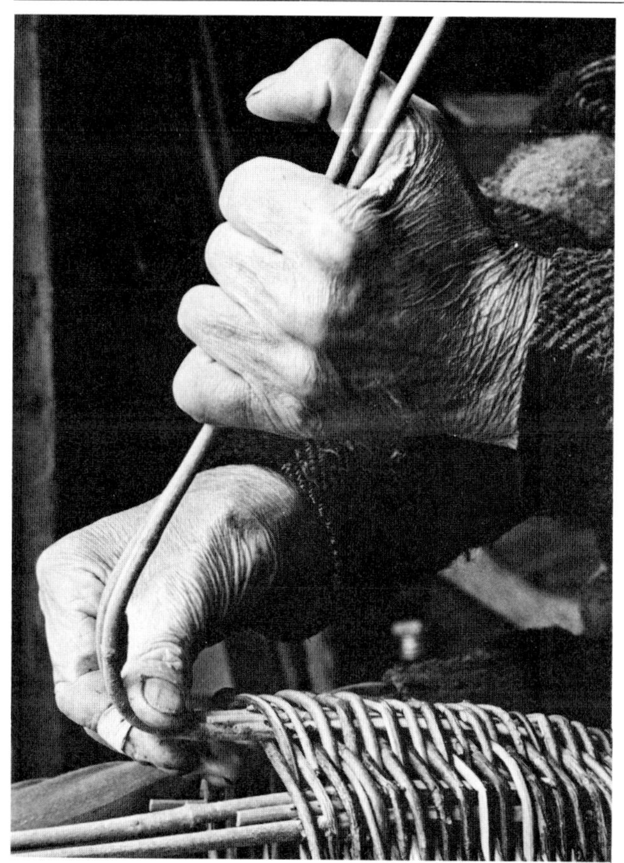

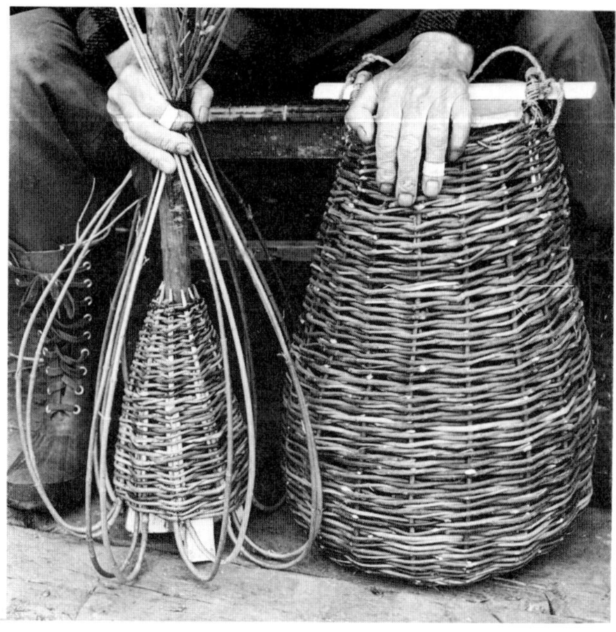

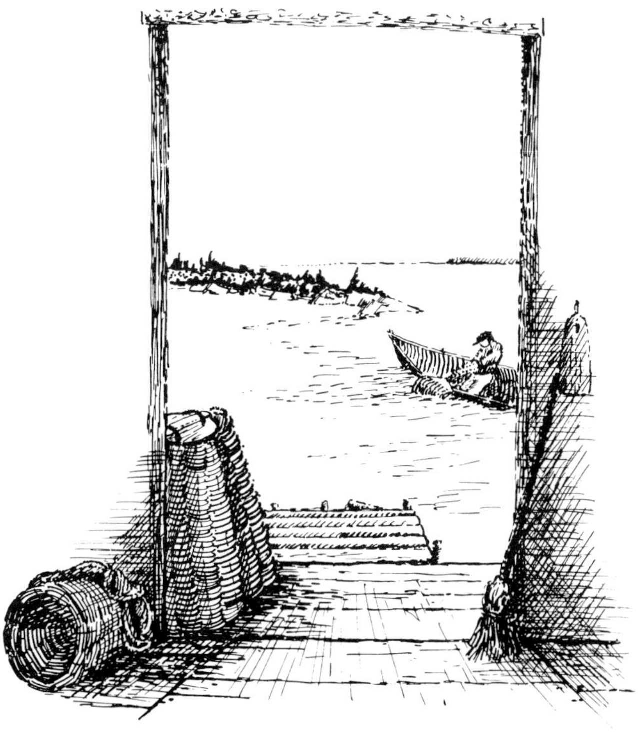

The craft of weaving eelpots and baskets, using the pliable stalks of the witherod bush, most likely came to Nova Scotia with German and English settlers in the middle of the eighteenth century. At that time, this particular style of fishtrap and basket was widespread in Great Britain and in northern and western European countries. In the Old Country, the weavers used various kinds of willow (*Salix*). When they came to Nova Scotia, they found little if any willow growing here but soon discovered that the stalks of the witherod bush, *Viburnum cassinoides*, were pliable like the willow. Out of these stalks could be fashioned baskets for garden gathering, collecting cod livers on the fishing schooners and the eel traps set in the brackish streams and ocean bays.

In Nova Scotia today, there are two main areas of witherod basketry: in a few Eastern Shore fishing communities where men weave eel traps and in Lunenburg County communities where men weave garden baskets, laundry hampers and eel traps.

There appear to be two methods of constructing the eel trap, which is a baited, double-funnel-shaped trap set with the mouth facing downstream. A few trap-makers on the Eastern Shore weave both funnels on warp elements inserted into a square piece of wood with a hole cut in the middle for the mouth of the trap. Other trap-makers do not use this piece of wood. After weaving the smaller funnel on a wooden mould, long pieces of withe are inserted into the weave and then bent up to form the warp network of the outer, larger part of the trap. After swimming through the opening, the eels are caught in the central chamber, from which they are removed through a wooden door in the other end of the trap (see the smallest photograph of Victor Bush).

The basketmakers of Lunenburg County tend the witherod bushes carefully, cutting the first year's growth for smaller baskets and the second and third year's growth for larger, heavier ones. The withes are usually cut in the fall and winter, when the leaves are off the bushes and the sap is in the roots. They can be cut at other times of the year, but as Bernie Mossman says, "They're a little more messy."

Like the eel traps, garden-gathering baskets are made in two stages. The bottom is woven first by inserting three withes, or "sticks," through a centre slit cut in each of three other sticks of the same length. The length of these sticks equals the diameter of the finished basket. The sticks are bound together in the centre and then radiated out to form the warp elements of the bottom of the basket; a piece of twine tied around each end holds them in position. They are woven with pairs of finer withes which are twisted once in a clockwise direction between each warp element.

When the bottom is complete, long pieces of withe are inserted into the weave of the bottom, one on each side of each warp element. These are gathered together and tied to form the side warp elements of the basket. Shape is given to the sides by tying a length of cord from the centre of the basket bottom to the knot holding the side withes together. The sides are woven, again using pairs of withes, and the top is finished by interweaving the side-withes back down into the last row. To raise the basket off the ground, and so prevent rot, a rim is woven around the bottom. Handles are added last, either two short ones, one on each side, or a long one stretching across the basket. They are made with stout pieces of withe driven down into the weave of the basket and bound with twine.

Withes are usually woven with the bark on the stalks, the weavers being careful to keep the baskets dry to prevent rot caused by "wit worms" living in the wet bark. Occasionally, the men will peel the withes and weave their womenfolk laundry hampers and very pretty yarn and sewing baskets.

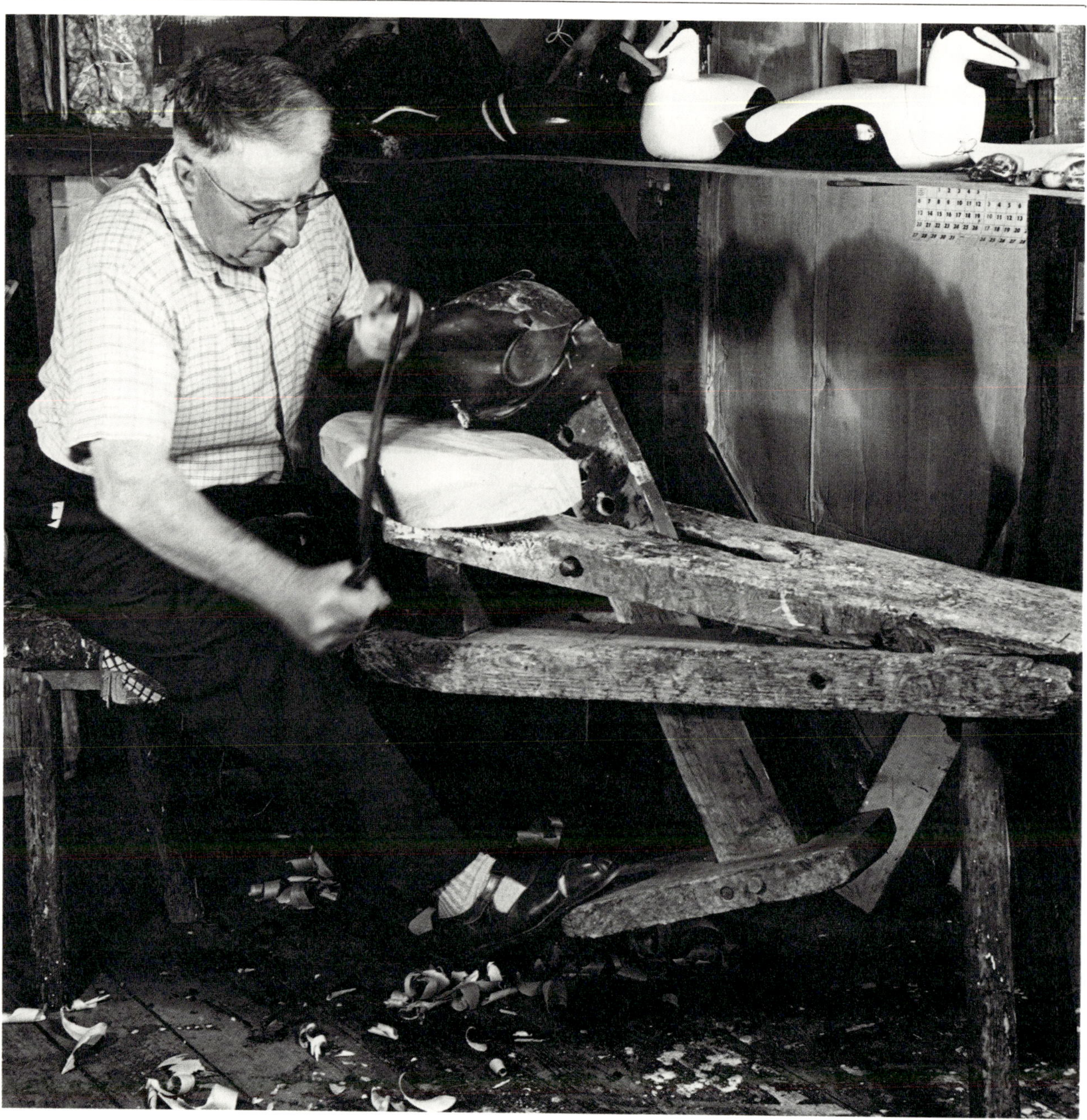

Perlus Finck

Born 26 June 1903, Decoys

You take back in the thirties, there was no way of gettin' any money. An' then, why, if a feller wasn't lazy, we'd go for a mess o' birds. We never made a practice of goin' an' gettin' them to sell or just for sport. Nothin' like that. Just get some to eat. An' for different birds, you'd need different decoys. Cedar seems to make the best decoy . . . fir is all right but cedar makes the best job . . . smooth. You get those old cedar poles. I have a pattern – rough the piece out an' then shave 'em down with a drawknife. Then sand 'em. The birds are all painted with enamel – the very best of paint. I've been makin' 'em ever since I was a boy.

Now I just whittle 'em for the pleasure of it. Just a hobby. It's different fellers around here make decoys, you know. An' some of 'em don't bother to make 'em good. It's like the old feller said, "A couple cuts wit' the axe an' they're finished." But I like to make anything half decent so it looks presentable. It takes time to do that. They got to be done right or they're not right. I probably do it the stupid way. I don't know. I like to make that kind o' stuff. Yes, you got to make 'em right. It's a funny thing, you know, but you take an interest into it an' you do the best you can wit' it an' you look at it. Well, it looks all right if the wood is worked right.

So, it's good fun doin' it. You make a lot o' friends – nice, good friends. A lot o' satisfaction. I give a lot away for ornaments, see. All kinds o' people visit me here in the run of a year. I like talkin' wit' people. I enjoy that.

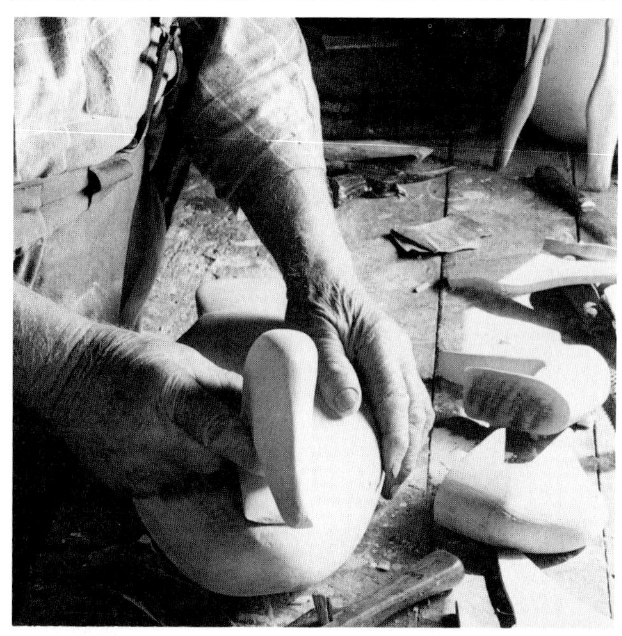

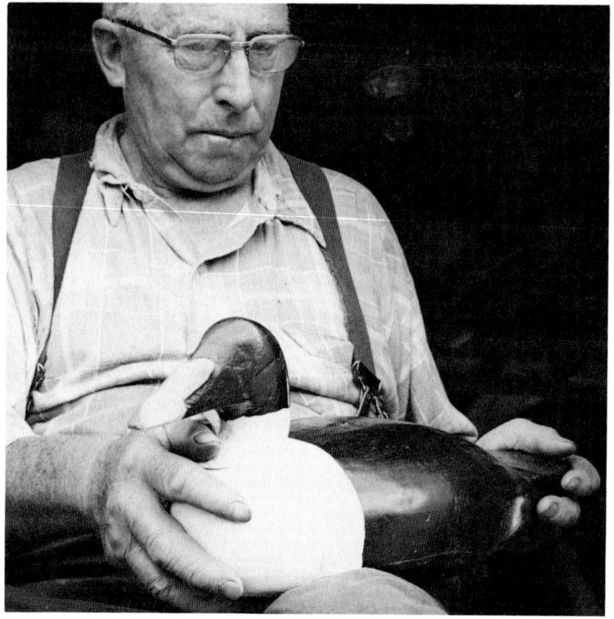

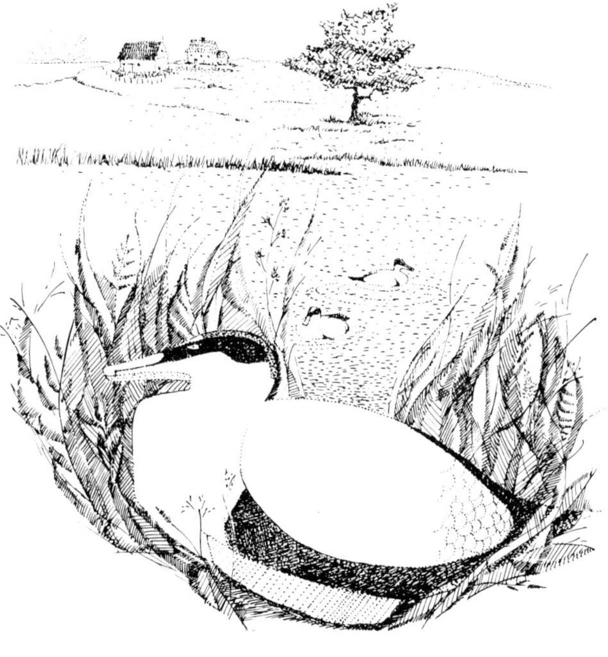

Through the ages, wild bird hunters have devised various methods of attracting the objects of the hunt. According to J. Barber, in his book *Wild Fowl Decoys*, English and Dutch hunters first used a V-shaped trap into which they drove the birds. This was called an "ende-kooy," after the Dutch expression. A later development was the arrangement of net-covered pipes leading off from an enclosed pond. Rather than driving the birds, they were enticed into the trap by trained dogs and semi-domesticated wild birds called "coy ducks."

In the latter half of the eighteenth century, when firearms came into general use, these trained birds were used to lure wildfowl to within firing range. It was also at this time that artificial birds, known as "decoys," began to be used in the hunt. America was being settled at this time, and written accounts record that live birds were never used here, only the decoys. Decoys were made from a wide range of materials: stuffed bird skins, feathers, mud, grasses, rushes, wood, cloth, leather, anything that could be tied or woven into a shape resembling the prey. By far, the wooden floating decoy was the most popular. To lure diving ducks, the hunters used "tollers," wooden decoys set out on a line, because diving ducks were known to "toll," or come in against the wind when landing on water.

Perlus Finck makes his wooden floating decoys in two sections. After drawing the body on a piece of wood, it is roughly cut out with a hatchet and then smoothed down with a drawknife and spokeshave. The head is carved with a jack-knife and is attached to the body with a five-inch galvanized pin through the neck. The decoy is then given a coat of enamel paint with markings characteristic of the bird it is imitating, and a lead keel is attached to the underside to give it weight and stability.

On East Ironbound Island in the 1930s, the men hunted eider and black ducks as a food source. Ironbound is about a mile and a half off the coast of Nova Scotia, and the duck-feeding grounds are on the seaward coast of the island, in six to fourteen fathoms of unsheltered Atlantic Ocean. To reach this area, the men devised a "duck tub," a small bathtub-shaped box, clinker-built with hinged wing-boards around the sides. "Well, I tell you, the tub is just big enough that when you sit down, you can just peep over the top, an' then the birds come up just as handy as you want 'em... they'll come up right against you, if you let 'em."

In the early morning, before daylight, the tub was dragged out into position by a dory, moored with a graplin line and two "dummy rocks," each on one and a half fathoms of line under the tub. The lines of decoys were set in place with one line of twelve windward tollers on the graplin line, three leeward lines of twelve tollers each, twenty-two fixed tollers on the wing-boards and eight loose decoys on the frame. The gunner shot to leeward as the birds came in against the wind, and his mate in the dory downwind picked up the birds as they floated towards him.

Duck hunters in Canada and the United States employed many kinds of rigs (batteries, sink pens, etc.), but this duck tub design appears to have been peculiar to the South Shore of Nova Scotia. The men who have hunted in such tubs assure us they feel quite safe, even in heavy weather, floating at eye-level with the broad Atlantic.

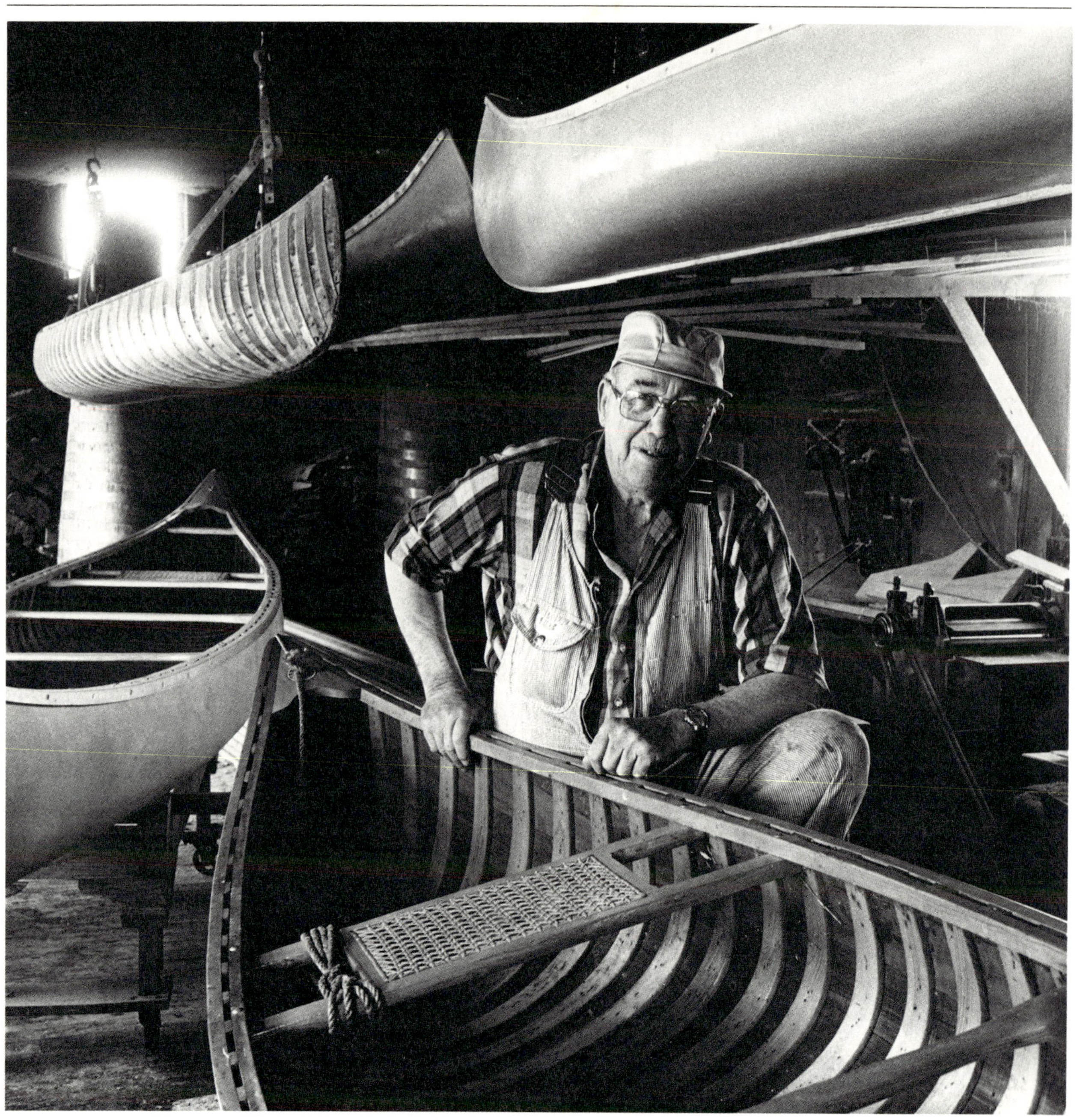

Harold Gates

Born 10 August 1906, Canoes

How did I learn? That's a good question. I just thought I could. I had to have a canoe an' the only way I could have one is to build it. I couldn't afford to buy one. I was always in the woods trappin' on the river an' a canoe is the best way to travel, so I figured the only way I could get one is to build it . . . an' I been buildin' ever since. I never followed a book or anythin'. I don't think that you . . . well, in books you'll see once in a while, a plan of a canoe. But I never thought that they was ever so good you know. No. I designed an' redesigned . . . kept buildin' 'em an' buildin' 'em. I'm not a marine architect, an' I done a lot o' reworking. There is a lot to figure up, to take into consideration . . . the good ones came in later years.

I design a canoe to serve a purpose, to work out of . . . a canoe that is stable. If you're in the woods, you just don't want an unstable canoe, so you design it so it would take a fair decent load and still be quite stable. It's like a dory, you know, it gets more stable as you load it. A lot o' factory-made canoes is servin' the purpose they're built for. You know, a lot o' people has got a cottage an' they probably only paddle their canoe up an' down the lake a half dozen times in the summer. Fibreglass or aluminum, you shove it under the cottage an' that's good until next year. And, of course, they're cheaper than wood. But they're no good in the woods. Fibreglass is rigid . . . no give. It's like a glass bottle . . . it's absolutely no give. Wood has got life an' some give to it. I'll take the wood.

You know, I get a lot of enjoyment out of it. I'm retired now an' if I just sit down I ain't goin' to be here long. I got to keep busy, I got to have somethin' on my mind . . . that I got

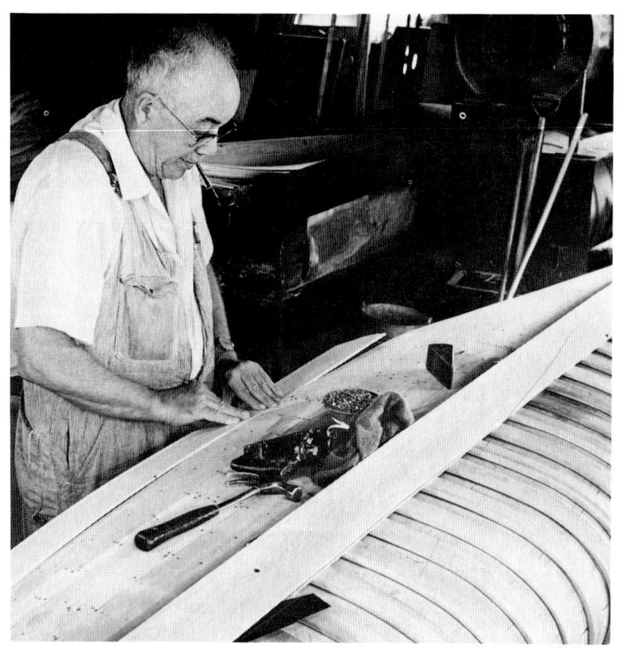

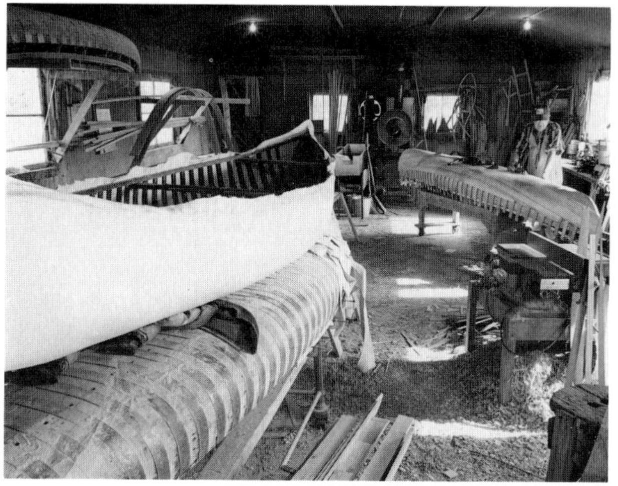

to do. Probably I can't do the work I used to do . . . not as fast an' I don't . . . well, I work six days a week. Maybe a little on Sundays but . . . about eight hours does me. Oh, there's days you feel good an' you'll get a lot done. An' there's days you don't feel so good . . . I got an old chair in the workshop. I can set down an' smoke awhile. Some feller will come by to talk . . . I don't have too much schoolin', but when a feller comes here to talk, well I can talk all day about canoes. Not much else maybe . . . but canoes . . . canoes is my life you might say.

When speaking of cedar-canvas canoes made in Nova Scotia, the names Tim Stewart and Harold Gates are synonymous. Tim Stewart (1877-1952) was born in Nova Scotia and learned to make canoes while working for a factory in Peterborough, Ontario. Not content with their designs, he came home and set up his own workshop in an old carding mill in South Brookfield, Queens County. He began to produce some very fine canoes and soon became well known for his genius with wood and for the perfection of his craft.

After Tim Stewart died, Harold Gates began making canoes on two moulds built by his late canoe-making friend. Like his predecessor, Harold applies the same standard of excellence in his work. All Stewart and Gates canoes have a decal of a floating swan on their bow.

When first designing a canoe, a quarter-model of the finished boat is made. From this model, the dimensions are measured and the mould is built: "You got to be right on the button with the model to get the mould right... whittle it out, cut it into sections, get the cross section measurements and scale them up to build your mould." Harold admits that the main secret in making a successful canoe is the shape of the mould. "Once you got the mould, anybody can build a canoe," he says modestly.

The mould is laid upside down on a worktable, and the canoe is built over it, putting the stems on first, then the ribbing and the planking and, finally, the gunnels: "The ribbing is white cedar and the planking is both white and red cedar... the gunnels are spruce and the thwarts and the seat wood is ash." All are carefully chosen for their different strengths and pliabilities.

The canoe is taken off the mould before canvassing: "The canvas is all one piece... you want to get it as dry as you can... you don't want any dampness in it whatsoever, for once you put the filler on, and paint it, if you ever got it out in the sun, the heat'll give you a slack canvas. I make my own filler with boiled oil, turpentine and driers; you can use chalk or whiting... paint it on with a brush and smooth it down with your hand to fill in all the pores in your canvas. And the last step is painting it–oil paint."

Harold Gates has been very interested in the older Micmac canoe designs documented in such books as *The Bark Canoes and Skin Boats of North America*, by E. T. Adney and H.I. Chapelle, and *Rushton and His Times in American Canoeing*, written by A. Manley. He has used Micmac lines to build a traditional birchbark canoe, as well as some very beautiful cedar-canvas canoes.

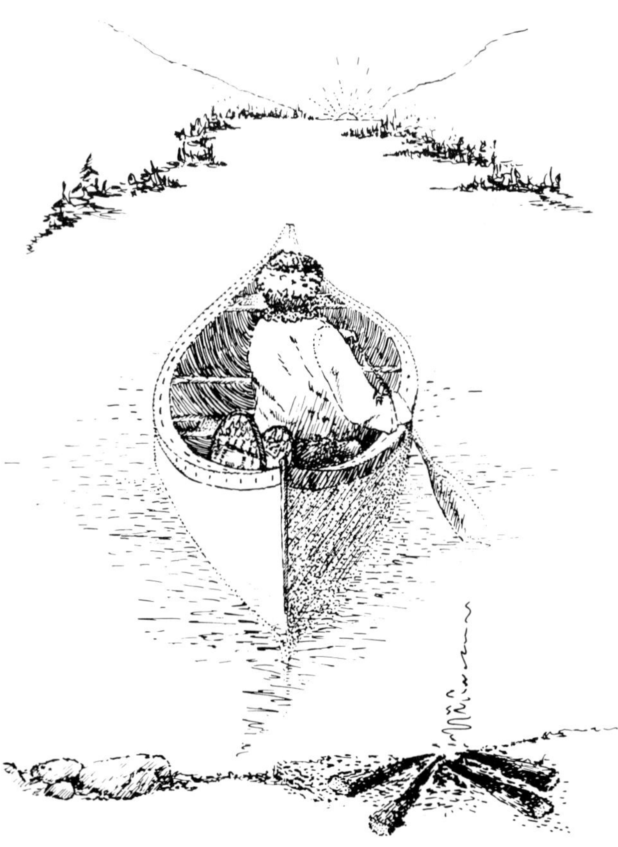

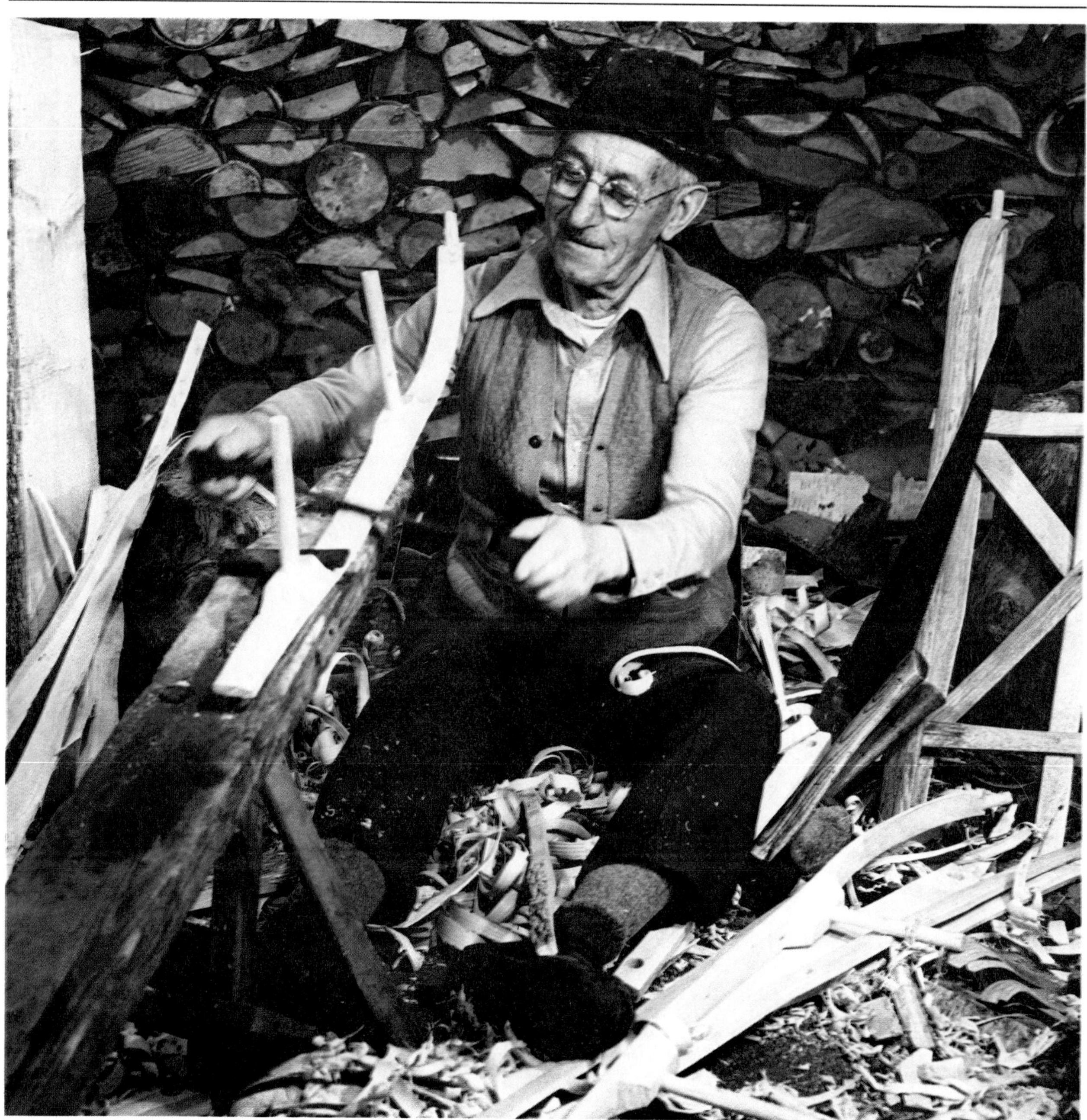

Durward Tupper

Born 16 February 1902, Shingle Sleds

Grandfather, he lived out on the mountains, you see . . . lived to be eighty-eight years old. Now my father died when I was seven, so I just took up with grandfather . . . an' followed him along . . . trappin' an' huntin' in the woods. He used to have what he called a shingle sled. We'd haul what we got – moose meat, a deer, pelts – on one of them sleds, you see . . . whatever we got. Haul that out on a small sled like the one I'm makin' here.

They've been in existence around here for many years. But now nobody makes 'em anymore. I imagine they was Indian-made in the first of it. They're all wood . . . ash . . . there was no metal in 'em. The pieces is all held together with little wooden pins. It's funny, you'd think that they would pull hard, but they don't. They go right over the snow. If you take a hundred pounds on these – maybe two hundred – if the snow ain't too soft, with snowshoes on, you can walk right along with it.

Those older fellers, if they was puttin' up a house or a barn, they'd go into the woods an' they'd cut trees down, you see . . . an' they would split out shingles an' tie 'em up an' put 'em on these sleds an' haul 'em home. Split 'em right in the woods an' haul 'em home. Shave 'em out after they'd get home. Grandfather, he always called 'em shingle sleds. I suppose they was bigger than what I make now. Six feet long maybe . . . one feller pulled an' the other feller pushed. Somethin' like a dog-sled they was . . . but they've been gone for years. There's a few trappers around yet that uses the small ones, an' they get after me to make 'em one. 'Course most of the people could make 'em if they wanted to – imagination is all you need.

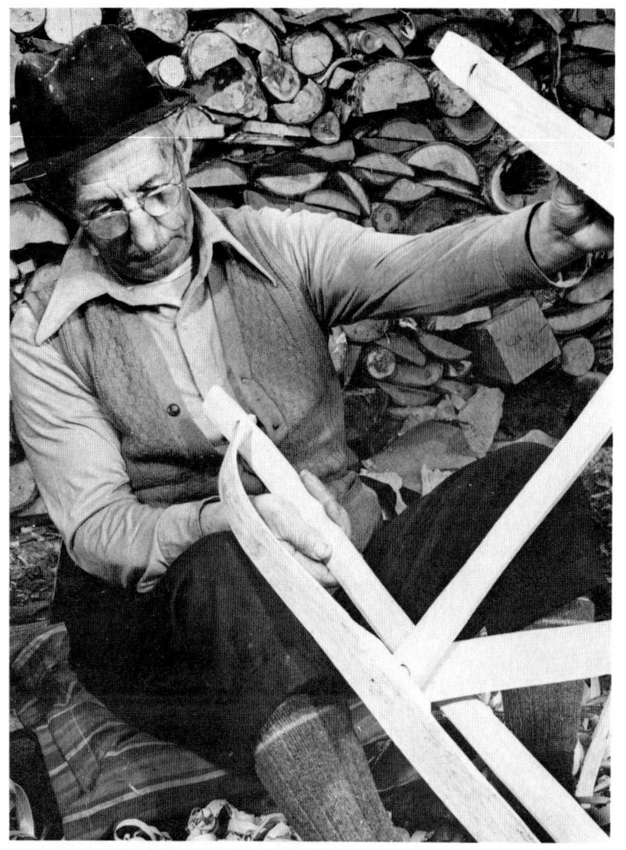

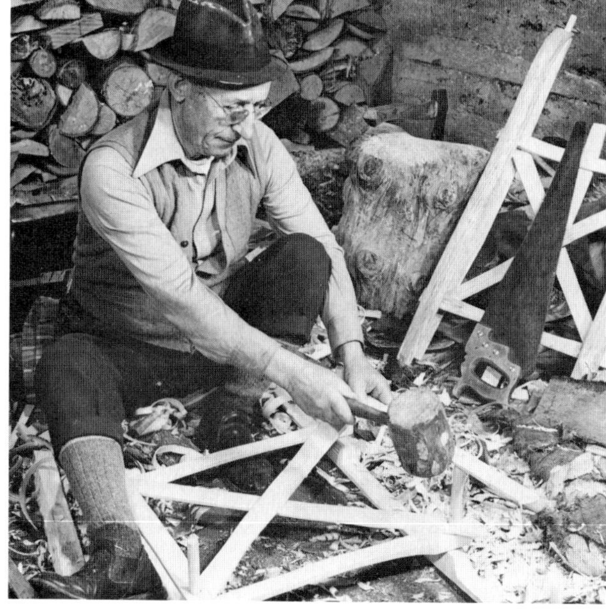

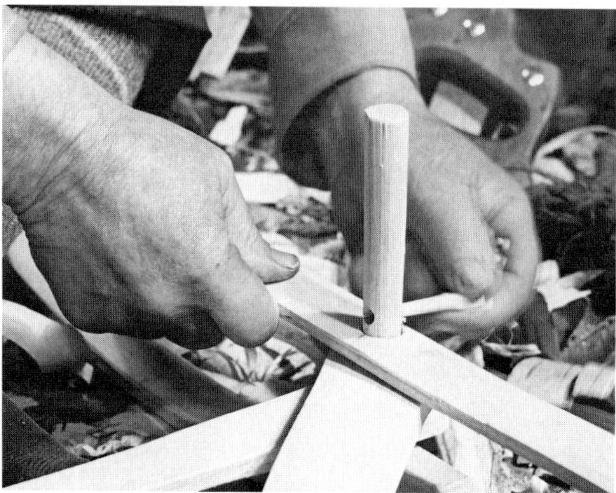

Durward Tupper learned how to make sleds by watching his grandfather and the other older men of his community who, in turn, claimed they learned the craft from the Micmac Indians. The age of the design is uncertain. Early European accounts of the Micmac people mention wooden sleighs. C. LeClercq, for example, in *New Relation of Gaspesia*, originally published in 1691, described "tabagannes" used by Micmac women for hauling household goods over the snow. Another Micmac word for sled was "Tobakun," recorded by Silas Rand in his English-Micmac dictionary. Indeed, the word "tabagin" is still used by the Micmac people today to refer to a wooden sleigh not too dissimilar to the shingle sled. This type of sleigh is described in "A Visit with Jack Sam Hinkley," published in the *Cape Breton Magazine*.

Durward Tupper's sleds are completely made of ash, and the pieces are held together by ash pins. "You cut your ash green and the quicker you use it, the better. In the winter until the leaves come out, why, that's the best time to cut your wood. You get a long, good straight piece of wood and split the runner and the shoe out of that piece, with the runner on the outside... just scrape off the bark an' that will get hard an' shiny, an' you can drag 'em right across the ground a lot easier." The runners are wide, usually three to four inches. The wood between the posts is cut away with an axe and chisel. Two sets of crosspieces, one running at right angles to the runners, the other making a cross in the centre, have holes cut in each end which fit over the posts.

Sometimes, Durward adds another piece in between the centre crosspieces to run parallel with the runners; it is pegged at each end with the right-angled crosspieces. Finally, the upper part of the runners are fitted over the posts and pegged.

The whole sled can be unpinned and carried as a bundle into the woods and then assembled when needed. The lightness of the wood and the width of the runners make the sled very easy to haul. In use, the sled is usually pulled from a man's shoulders by means of ropes or straps.

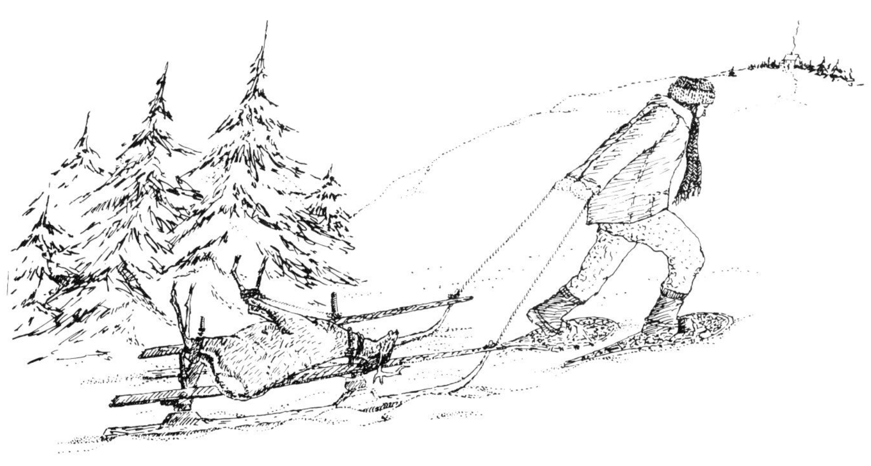

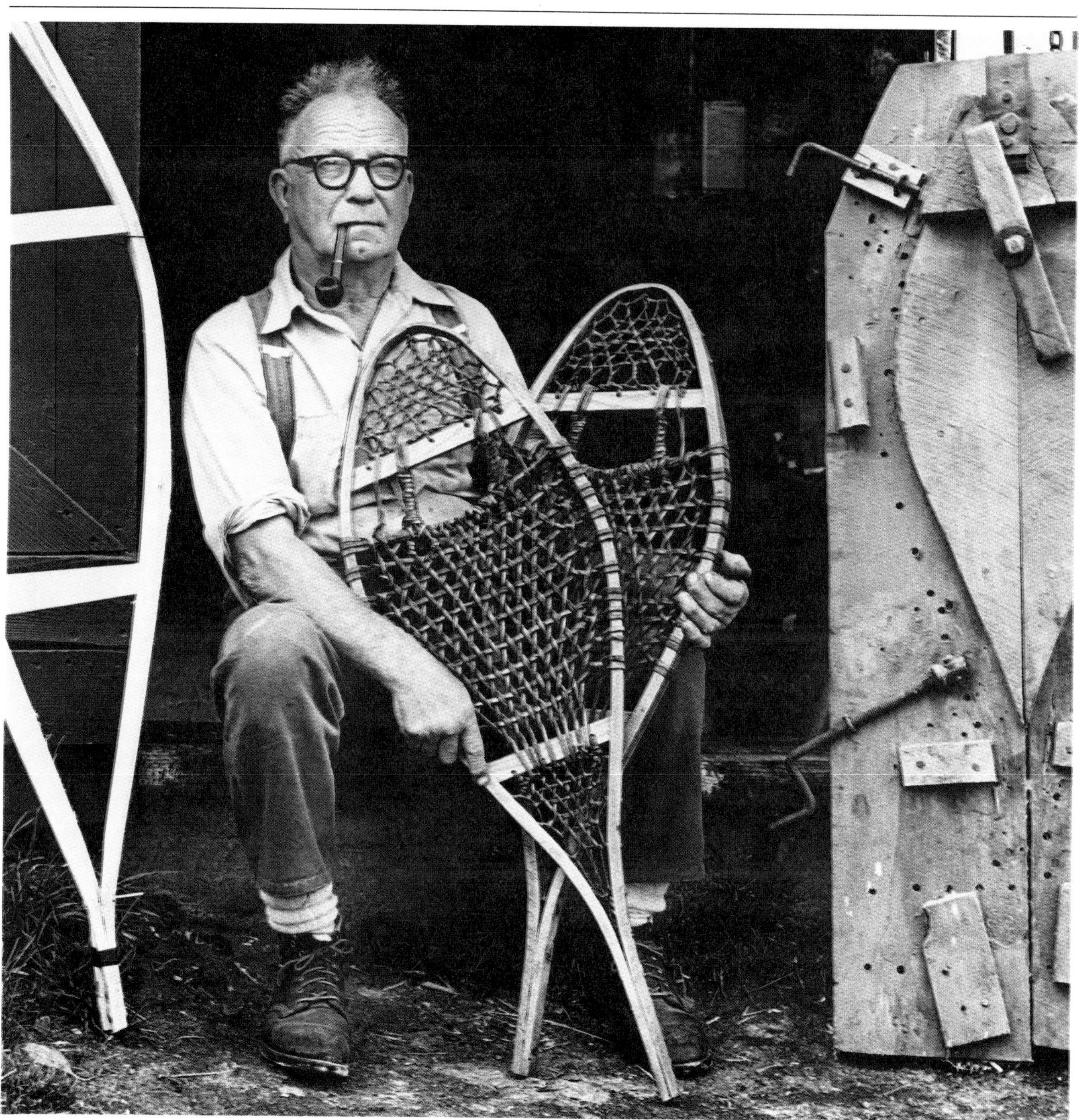

Wilson Sarty

Born 9 February 1906, Snowshoes

It's more to makin' snowshoes than meets the eye. It doesn't look like much work, but it's really quite a job. I make 'em right from scratch. The best frame you can get is to go into the woods to cut your own wood – ash, oak – a good hard wood. You pick out your tree that you think will make a good pair of snowshoes. Your wood has got to be about six inches in the round and eight feet long. An' you split that in half an' then quarter it. From there you work down inch by inch and bend it onto the mold.

Now the lacin' . . . that's taken from cowhide. Some people lace 'em in nylon an' some kind of fishin' line, but I like the rawhide. I don't know if it's really superior to some o' the modern lacin's or not, but it's the old Indian tradition an' that's what I like to follow. 'Course it's more work – you got to soak it an' scrape the hair off, cut it into strips. . . . The first pair . . . I wanted a good pair of snowshoes an' I figured that if I made 'em myself, they'd be good. I found it quite a job to lace 'em . . . took me about six months to get the hang of it. See, the way it's done – if you had a strip long enough, a snowshoe can be laced with that one strip. An' every twist that you make in lacin' has to be in the right place. If you make one twist wrong, it throws the whole t'ing out. The hardest part in makin' a pair of snowshoes is the lacin'. Sometimes, when I was first started, I would have a snowshoe almost complete an' somewheres about halfways through I made a mistake – made one mistake, one twist the wrong way. Then I had to take the whole t'ing – if I wanted to make a good job of it – I'd have to take the whole lacin' out an' start again. There'd be some bad words flyin' around for a while! Oh, I was determined.

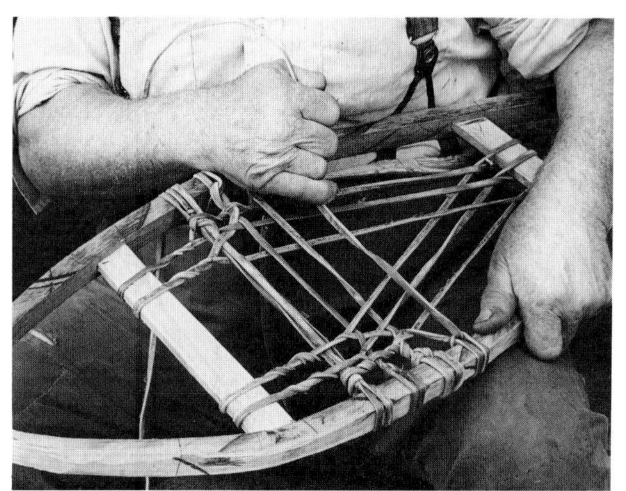

See, I made 'em for myself – use 'em on my trapline an' for hunting in the winter. I do . . . I get satisfaction out of somebody lookin' at a pair o' my snowshoes an' sayin', "Well, there is somethin' nice." But then maybe they don't look perfect to me! If you make somethin' an' say, "This is as far as I can go, I can't do no better," you run into trouble. You tend to slip the other way instead of improvin' it. I often think that once I make a perfect pair o' snowshoes – one that suits me – I don't think maybe I'll make another one. I haven't made a perfect pair yet – not to my way o' thinkin'.

According to W. Osgood and L. Hurley in their manual, *The Snowshoe Book*, archaeologists have been unable to date the origin of either skis or snowshoes, although there is some evidence to suggest that they may have originated in the snowy districts of central Asia about 4000 B.C. Thus, the authors say, "... the snowshoe/ski is one of the oldest inventions of man." Asian peoples migrated east and west, and it is interesting to note that the ski became the favoured means of winter travel in northern Asia and Europe, while the snowshoe was adopted by the North American Indians for winter travel in their temperate woodland home.

In the Maritime Provinces, where the woods are dense and the snowfall is not quite heavy enough to cover the rocky terrain, short snowshoes like the bear-paw and the standard types are preferred. The frame of the snowshoe is split from green wood with the bark side on the outside of the frame. The wood is steamed, and while it is still hot it is fitted into a mould. Wilson Sarty explains that "If you bend it after steaming while it is still green, it will hold that shape much better than if you took dry wood an' wet it, an' steamed it, an' bent it. The green wood you have to leave in the mould for about a week; but if it's dry wood, a coupl'a days should dry it out."

Once the wood is dry, holes are drilled between the toe and the heel for lacing the "lanyard," or inside webbing. The lacing is traditionally leather: beaver, moose, caribou and cowhide, all have been used in the past. Unlike Wilson Sarty, many snowshoe-makers today prefer synthetic neoprene, because of its strength and the fact the mice don't like to eat it. The lacing patterns are complicated, and as Wilson Sarty points out, "Every snowshoe-maker has a different way of lacin'."

Once the frames are made and laced, a pair of foot bindings is added. Trappers wear shoes without heels, because they find that the heels tend to cut into the leather bindings and lacings. As Wilson says, "One secret in makin' a pair of snowshoes, you have to keep 'em balanced right. You have to have the heel heavier than the toe, for when you lift your foot up to take a step, the heel should drag, not the whole foot come up. If you don't get 'em balanced just right, they're awkward things to walk in."

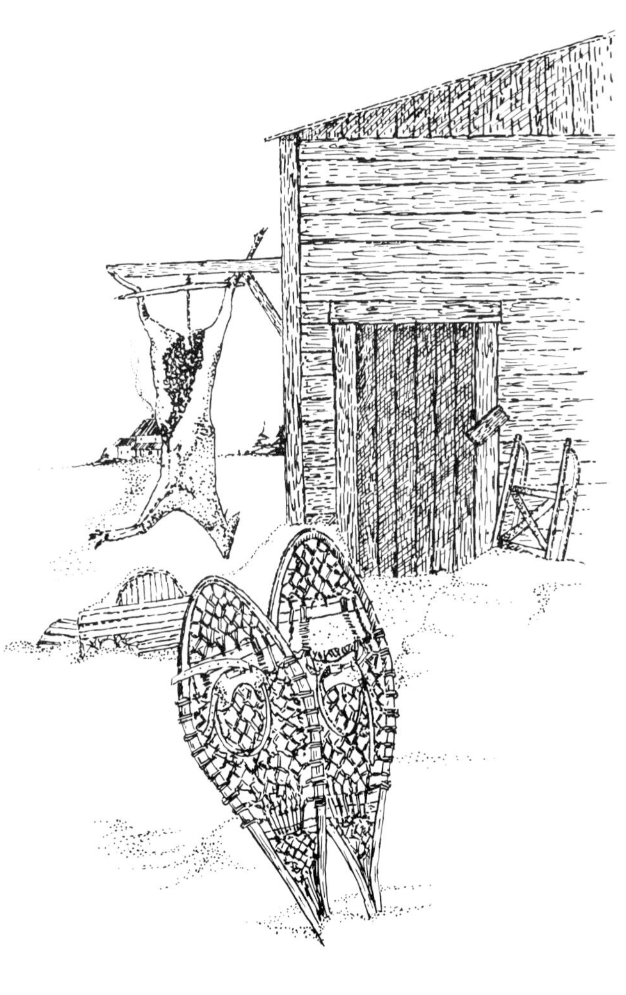

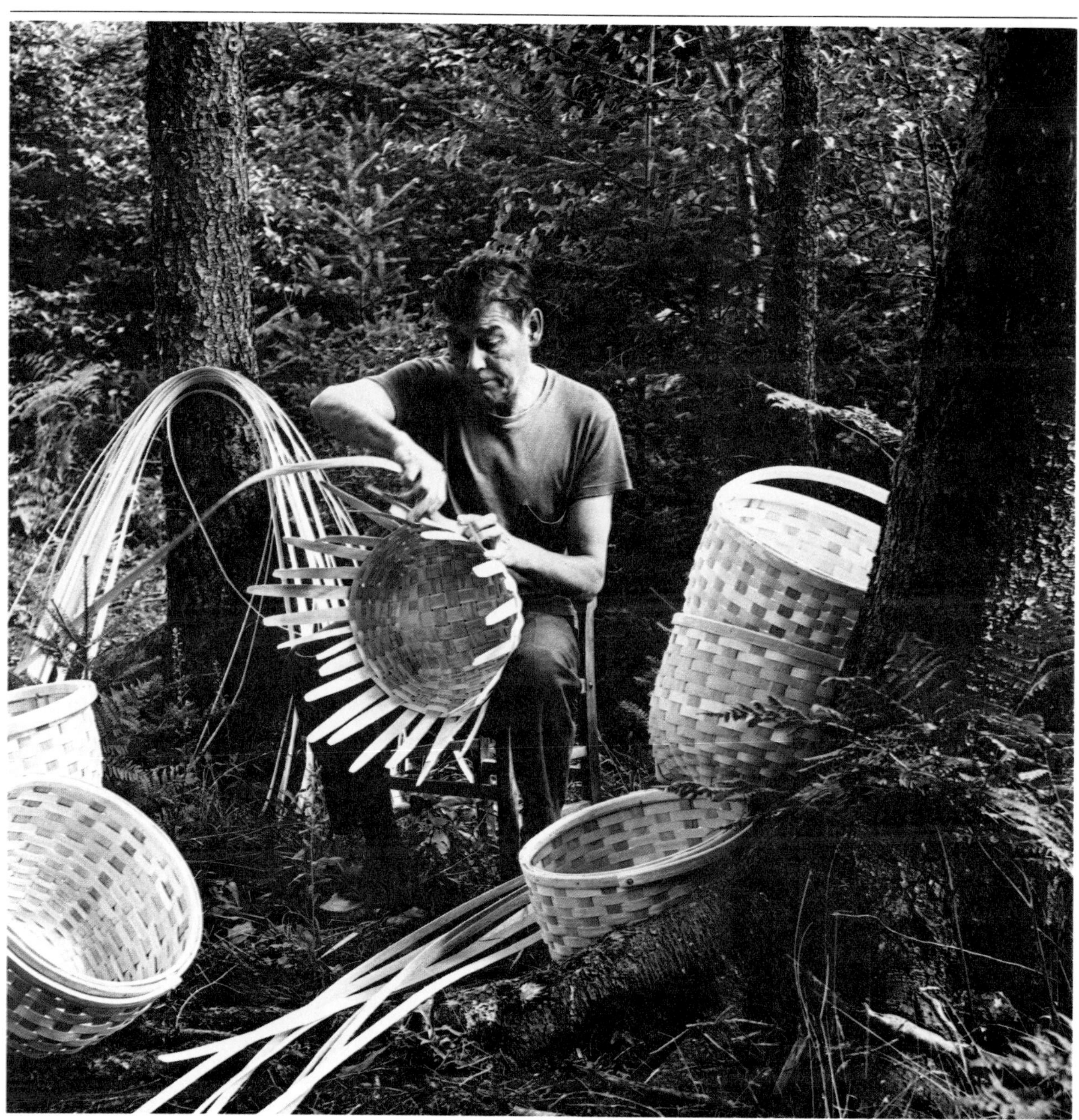

Noel Smith

Born 10 May 1917, Apple/Potato Baskets

These baskets are for apples or potatoes – workin' baskets. Now you take the older folks, like the womenfolks, they used to make the fancy baskets. Fancy basket is like a shopping basket or one you'd use for a picnic basket. It won't be used so hard. All ash – only the fancy basket you take more care in the making of it. Now in the thirties, the apple basket is all they made in the Valley. They produced quite a pile of 'em. The apple farms don't use that many now. They got canvas baskets. When the war broke out, there was nobody there to make baskets, so they turned around an' they got canvas baskets an' they got likin' 'em so they kept on usin' 'em.

Now I don't see anyone else around makin' 'em except a white feller up on North Mountain there. He makes the same kind o' bottom as me – ash – but he fills 'em out with some kind o' nylon, half-inch nylon webbing for the sides. Him an' me . . . we're the only ones as far as I can tell.

I used to help the old man there, Frank Paul . . . he's dead now. He used to make baskets all the time, all year 'round. I was a little kid . . . I used to go get ash an' help him to nail handles. Once we went up to Bridgetown from Cambridge. An' we got off the train at . . . must o' been two o'clock in the afternoon. On a Saturday. No money. To tell you the truth, the old man didn't have no money or anything . . . had no food even. "What are we goin' to do? We got no money, no food."

"We'll have some," he says.

It was in the spring . . . we went right in the woods about five miles up the mountain there . . . got some ash, split it out, drawknifed it an' we pounded it out. We made half a

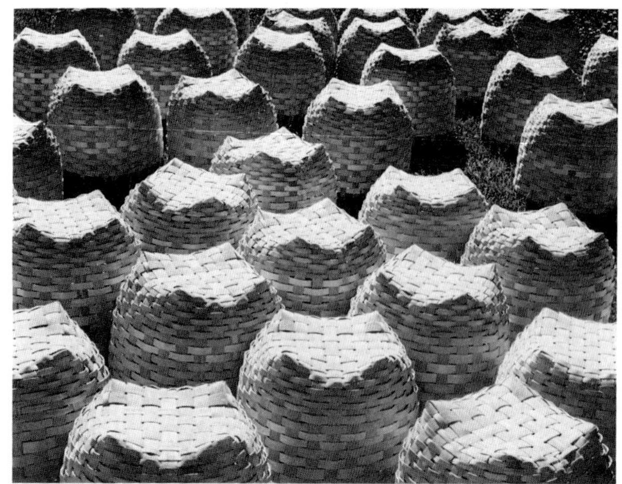

dozen baskets that day before night. We took 'em to town an' sold 'em. Store'd give you some money – thirty-five or forty cents each – an' then the rest, groceries. They wouldn't give you all money. An' then we went back into the woods an' made more baskets. That's the way we did it. We stayed, let me see, we must o' stayed a couple o' weeks. He knew the country an' he had been there before . . . he wanted to be in the woods where he could get the good ash. I knowed him since I was . . . all my life. I guess he got me interested in makin' baskets. An' now . . . well, there's a lot o' hard work to it, but you're your own boss.

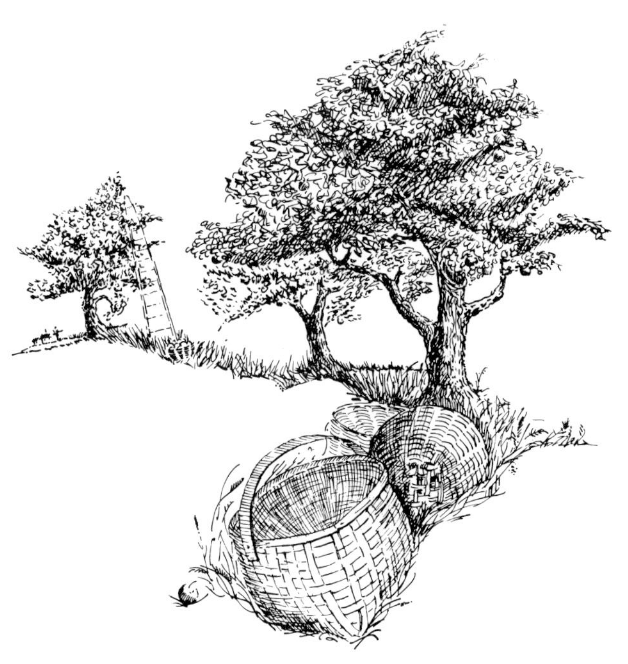

The apple baskets made by Noel Smith and his family are woven with a traditional checker weave. Ted Brasser of the National Museum of Canada, in his study, *A Basketful of Indian Cultural Change*, believes such baskets required the use of steel tools and were introduced to the Indians living in the lower Delaware River Valley about 1700 by Swedish and possibly German settlers.

In a recent publication from the Nova Scotia Museum, *Elitekey*, Ruth Whitehead shows that prior to European contact, the Micmac people knew how to use stone tools to make cedar splint linings for bark canoes, and that they also knew how to weave cedar bark strips in twill and checker weaves. In presenting this evidence, Whitehead recognizes that this does not necessarily imply that these techniques were combined in making baskets. However, artwork and manuscripts from the late eighteenth and early nineteenth centuries depict and refer to the Micmac Indians weaving splint baskets. The Micmacs were known to have travelled throughout the Maritimes, Quebec and New England, and Whitehead feels it is possible they could have brought splint basketry techniques to Nova Scotia by the end of the eighteenth century.

The introduction of European steel tools made it easier to produce wood strips from hardwood trees, and basketmaking using the checker-weave technique became an important source of income for many Indian families. Traditionally, the men cut the trees and prepared the wood, while both men and women did the weaving.

White ash, black ash, poplar, maple and birch are all used for basketmaking, although white ash is preferred because of its strength and colour. Noel Smith uses white ash in all his baskets, and he prepares the wood in the traditional Micmac way. The tree is felled and cut into eight-foot lengths. Each length is then halved, quartered and cut into smaller and smaller sectors (pie-shaped sections) until the desired width of the finished wood strip is reached. With a drawknife, the heartwood and the bark are removed and the sides are trimmed, so the pieces are rectangular in cross section.

The wood is now pounded. Ash grows very quickly, with a layer of porous membranes laid down between each year's growth. By pounding with a force perpendicular to the plane of the growth ring, this membranous layer can be broken down, thus separating the growth rings into long narrow pieces of wood known as "strips," "splints" or "splits." In years gone by, the wood was pounded with the blunt end of an axe, but more recently electric pounding machines have been used. The strips are separated again and again into progressively thinner layers by careful manipulation of a jackknife or a crooked knife. For fine baskets, the splints are cut into narrower strips with basketry gauges or "squaw knives," small tools with sharpened watch springs set into the wood at definite intervals.

The apple baskets have a square bottom in which the strips are interwoven in a plain under-one, over-one (checker) weave and then turned up to create the warp elements or "standards" for the sides of the basket. More strips, "weavers," are added, and they are woven through the standards in a checker pattern until the top of the basket is reached. The baskets are then left to dry upside down in the sun, and next day the rows of weaving are tamped close together with a hammer and a piece of wood. The standards lying on the inside of the uppermost weaver are cut off flush with the top of the basket. The standards lying on the outside of the uppermost weaver are sharpened to a point, bent over this last row of weaving and inserted into the inside weave of the basket. The rim and the handle are put on last.

In the plain basket, the rim consists of two pieces of ash bent to the shape of the basket opening, one on each side of the weave covering the top row of weaving. They are nailed together, while the handle is fastened with a screw on each side through the outer rim.

Noel and his family also weave fancy apple baskets, picnic baskets and fragrant sweet-grass baskets.

The older, more complex techniques are presently being revived under the direction of the Micmac Arts and Crafts Society in Antigonish.

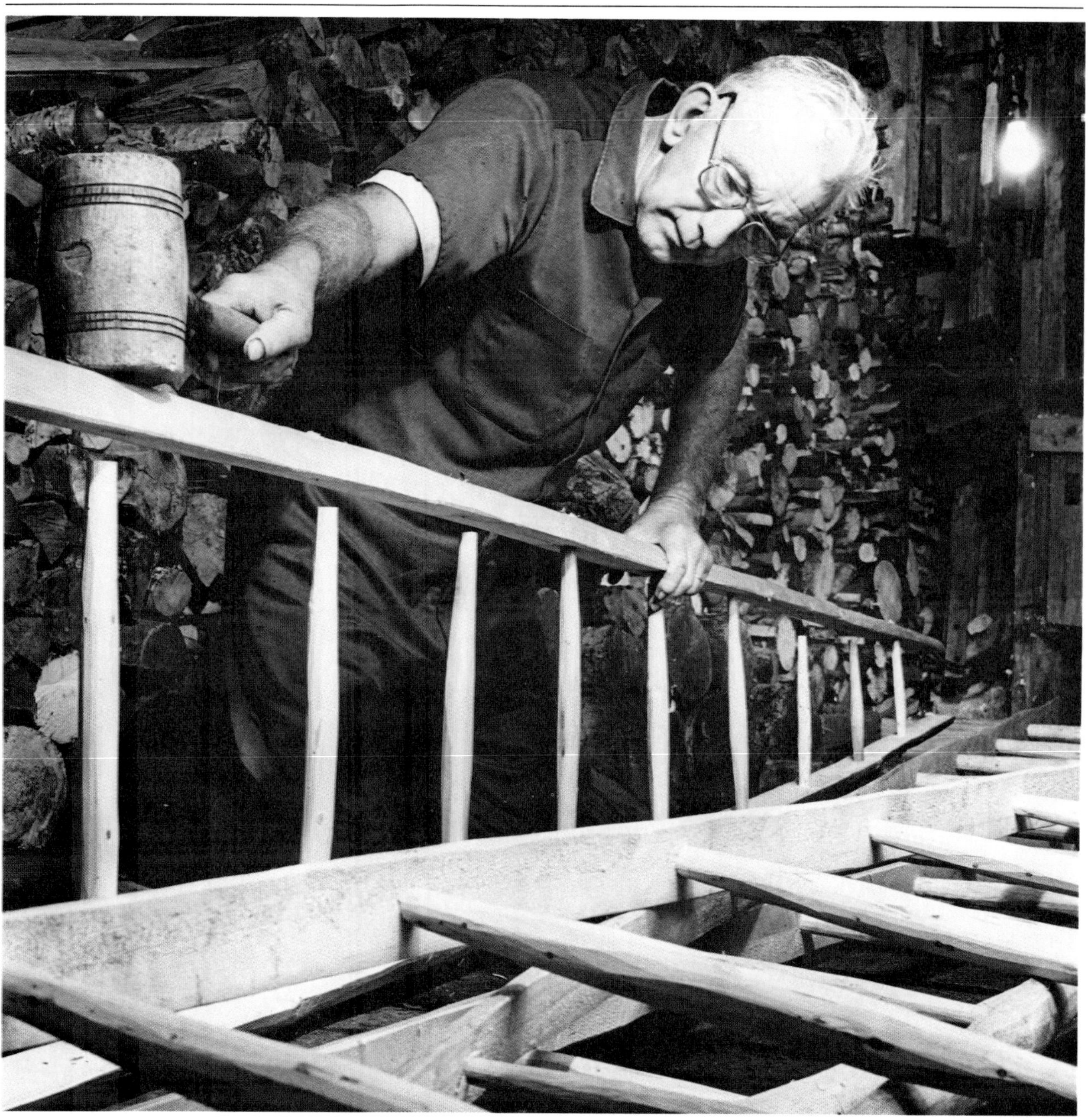

Ralph Mahar

Born 25 July 1911, Apple Ladders

Well, when I was a boy, in my middle teens, I figured I wanted a little bit o' spending money, so I went back in the woods an' cut a few alder poles an' carried 'em out on my back an' that's the start of my makin' ladders. I think it's coming' up now that I'm sellin' ladders to what would be the third generation since I started . . . third generation o' fellers on the same farm. Makes me feel as if I must be gettin' older! Don't know whether that's a nice feelin' or not. I've had people – it was two years ago – sold 'em ladders for years an' they said, "Well, I don't expect you to be around any more with ladders." I've been around two or three years since . . . but I have cut down in my ladder makin'. This year I'll be makin' a hundred an' twenty-five or so. Three years ago I made o'er three hundred.

Lots o' work to them ladders. The first thing . . . you got to try to inquire around an' find a place where you can go cut your ladder wood . . . round poles which you can find in thick groves o' spruce. Cut 'em, lug 'em out o' the woods, bring 'em home. Then shave the bark all off an' rip 'em in half through the centre lengthwise . . . you always keep your poles together so you don't get your sides mixed up – some might have a little different curve in them. They wouldn't make as good a ladder if they wasn't matched. An' my rungs . . . I always cut the small spruce that grows in groves. They grow tall. Lots o' them scrub spruce would be only one and a half inches across an' lots o' times they grow up twenty, twenty-five feet. My customers, they been accustomed to that kind o' rung. They really prefer it. With them hardwood rungs . . . well, in some instances, the hardwood

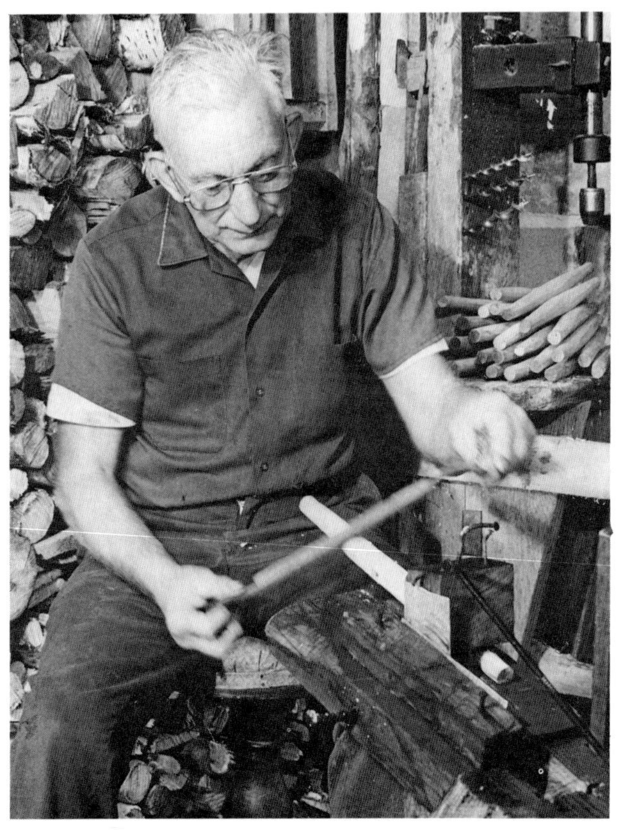

rung, when it gets wet, it's more slippery. You take lots o' times you go out pickin' in the mornin' an' there'd be a heavy dew an' the grass is wet an' your feet gets wet – an' on a hardwood rung, your feet is more apt to slip. Another thing . . . the spruce is lighter, an' it's strong.

Oh, there's a lot to it . . . I try to make a good ladder. I get pleased with 'em when I do a particular job. I sure do. I figure that's the way we were created in the beginning – for man to enjoy his work an' the work of his hands. I sure do enjoy my work.

The Annapolis Valley has long been known as an apple-producing region for the international export market. Over the years, the apple industry has supported many different craftsmen. In earlier times, the apples were shipped in wooden barrels which supplied work for many coopers, both in the Valley and in Lunenburg County. The Micmac Indian basketweavers are still providing the growers with bushel-sized gathering baskets, and the ladder-makers are still making the ladders.

The two sides of an apple ladder come to a point at the top, allowing it to be easily placed into the upper branches of a tree. The rungs, placed at one-foot intervals along the length of the ladder, gradually decrease in width from the bottom to the top.

Ralph Mahar has been making apple ladders for over fifty years, and he has noticed a few changes in the industry that have affected his craft: "When I first started makin' ladders; I made ladders as long as thirty-two feet. In them days, there were different varieties of apples grown – Baldwins an' Starks. Some of them old trees were tremendously big. They were like skyscrapers; you'd walk up ten, fifteen feet before you hit a limb... an' they would have as many as twenty-two barrels of apples on them. Now, they're finding it more practical, I understand, to grow the fruit on younger an' more lower trees, so twenty feet is about as long a ladder that you sell nowadays, an' not too many twenty-foot ladders... from fifteen- to eighteen-foot ladders is what really sells the best."

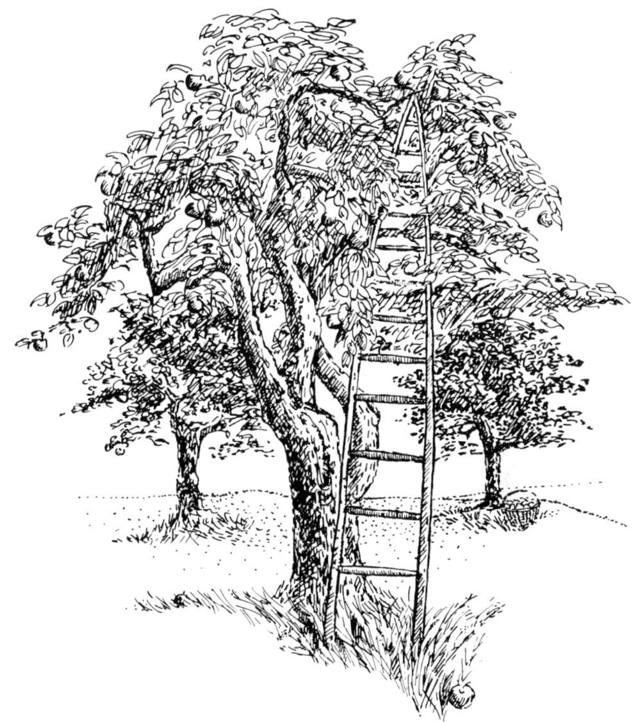

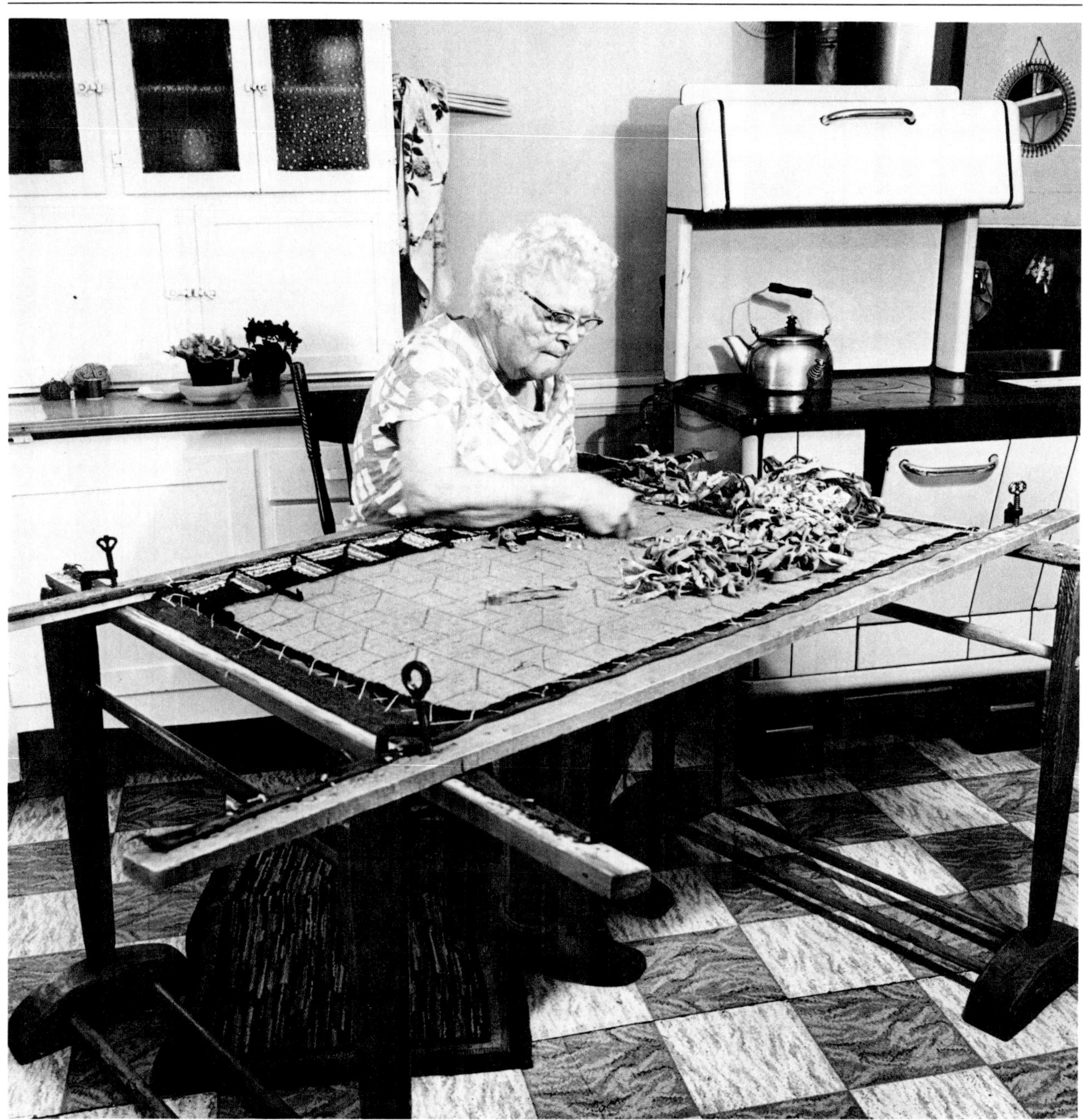

Anne Wile

Born 2 September 1895, Mat-Hooker

I grew up on a farm, an' there was plenty of work to do in the summers so we never hooked then. Hooked in the winters. Used an old sugar bag or somethin' for the backing an' there was no shortage of rags. You'd have your old clothes you wear out. Save them. That's where the rags comes from – old clothes. It was a big family – there was six girls of us an' two boys. We had rags enough – we had a rag barrel. An' we saved all the old clothes in that . . . we never wasted nothin'. An' all winter long we set an' we hooked an' hooked an' hooked. Mother an' me an' my sisters. It was fun.

I learnt from my mother an' she learnt from her mother. When I was young, I watched my mother an' followed her in her fashion when I could get hold of a hook. An' when I first started – oh, I guess I was twelve, thirteen years old – I just used to take a hairpin. An old hairpin and hook with that. An' when mother went to make the meals, why then I'd get her hook an' use that. Mother, I guess she didn't leave my hookin'. Not at first when I was just learnin' . . . she pulled it out if I was off to school or somethin'. Then when I was fourteen or so, I could hook on my own, an' we'd all hook together – sometimes on one mat – in the wintertime when the evenings was long. I hooked faster then than I do now – as you grow old, you slow up . . . that's for sure. I used to hook twelve or fifteen mats every winter. Last winter I hooked three. Them days all the women hooked. The floors was covered with mats to keep the cold out.

An' we used to trade 'em to a feller that come around – what we used to call the mat man. We'd trade away a good part of our nice new mats to him an' get oilcloth an' things like

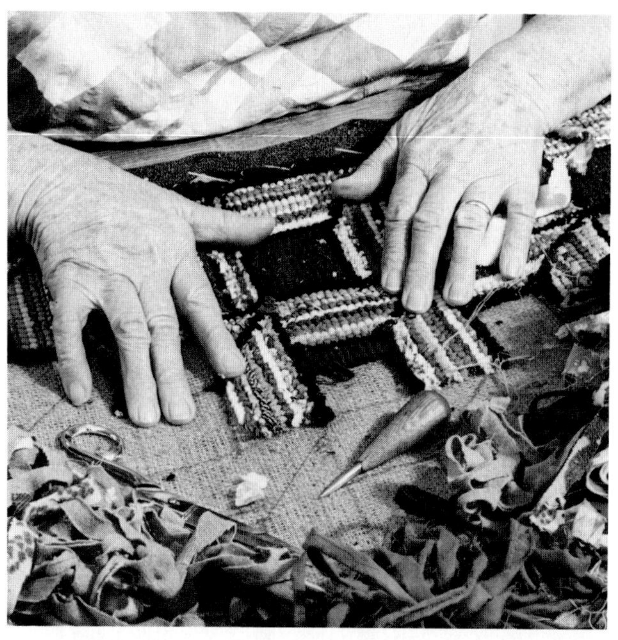

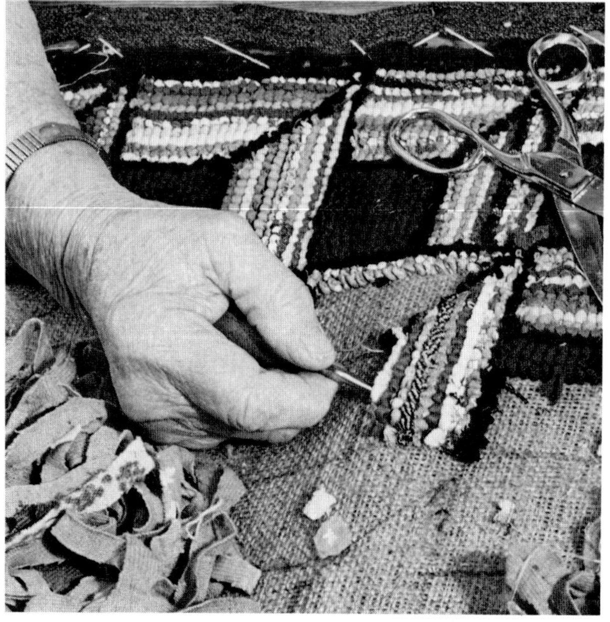

that . . . an' not much else. That cheap old oilcloth for the floors. We knew we wasn't getting anything for our mats, but we couldn't sell them an' we couldn't use all that we made – an' we could use the oilcloth. Farmers them days didn't have money to buy. . . well, that's the way it was home there. The mats was the things that had to go to get oilcloth.

But things has changed. I have three daughters. They don't want to hook. The older one can hook but she don't. She's got these wall to wall carpets you know!

Hooked rugs have been made in Nova Scotia for many years, and they are a prime example of the thriftiness and ingenuity of the people. When the rug-hookers gather in the wintertime, the contents of the rag barrel are cut into long narrow strips. If new material is not available, discarded burlap bags are used as backings, stretched on simple wooden frames. Some women draw their own mat designs freehand on the backing, others trace cups and saucers, or draw geometric shapes with a ruler. Still other hookers prefer to buy already stamped mat patterns, such as the ones which were produced by the John E. Garrett Company in New Glasgow from 1892 until very recently.

The mat pattern is hooked by holding a length of yarn or material strip at the back of the work with one hand and then inserting a small hook-shaped tool with the other hand through the backing material from the front of the work. The material is caught by the hook and pulled as a loop to the front of the work. The loops are pulled up as closely together as possible to create a thick pile and to prevent unravelling. The mats are finished by sewing a heavy material binding or crocheting a heavy yarn around the edges.

Rug-hooking is widely practised in Nova Scotia, and there are localized differences in styles and patterns. Mary Saunders, writing in *A Nova Scotia Workbasket*, shows that in the southwestern part of the province (Yarmouth, Digby), the women clip the loops giving the mats a soft, velvety texture, while in the South Shore communities of Queens and Lunenburg and in the Pictou, Cumberland and Colchester areas, the loops are usually left uncut. The Acadian hookers around Cheticamp, Cape Breton, occasionally sculpture their floral and scroll designs as they clip their mats.

Anne Wile is from Lunenburg County, and characteristic of hookers in this area she draws her pattern out in straight lines, following the lines of the weave in the backing material. The outlines of each square are hooked in black. Each square is divided in half diagonally, with a smaller square marked off at one end. This square is hooked in a solid colour, while the rest of the larger square is hooked vertically and horizontally in a "hit or miss" pattern with multi-coloured rags.

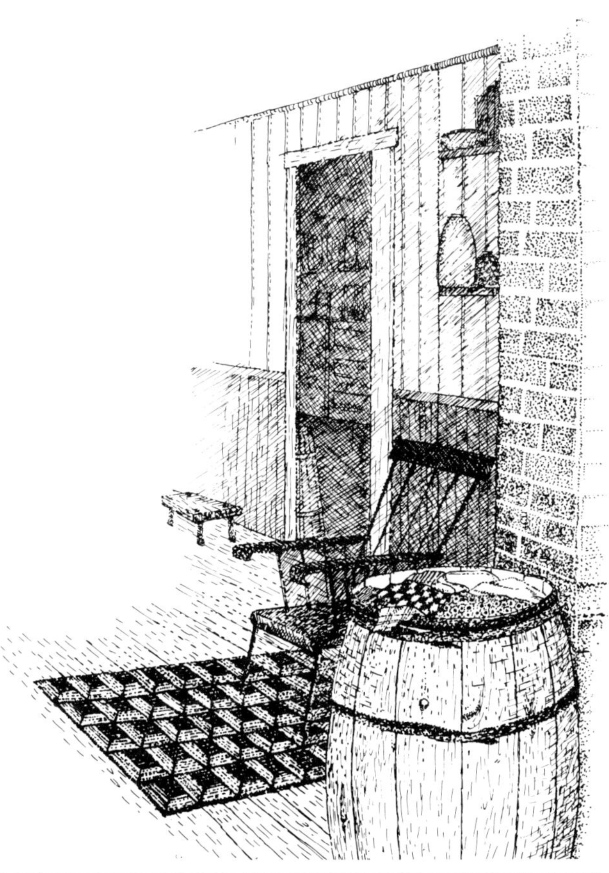

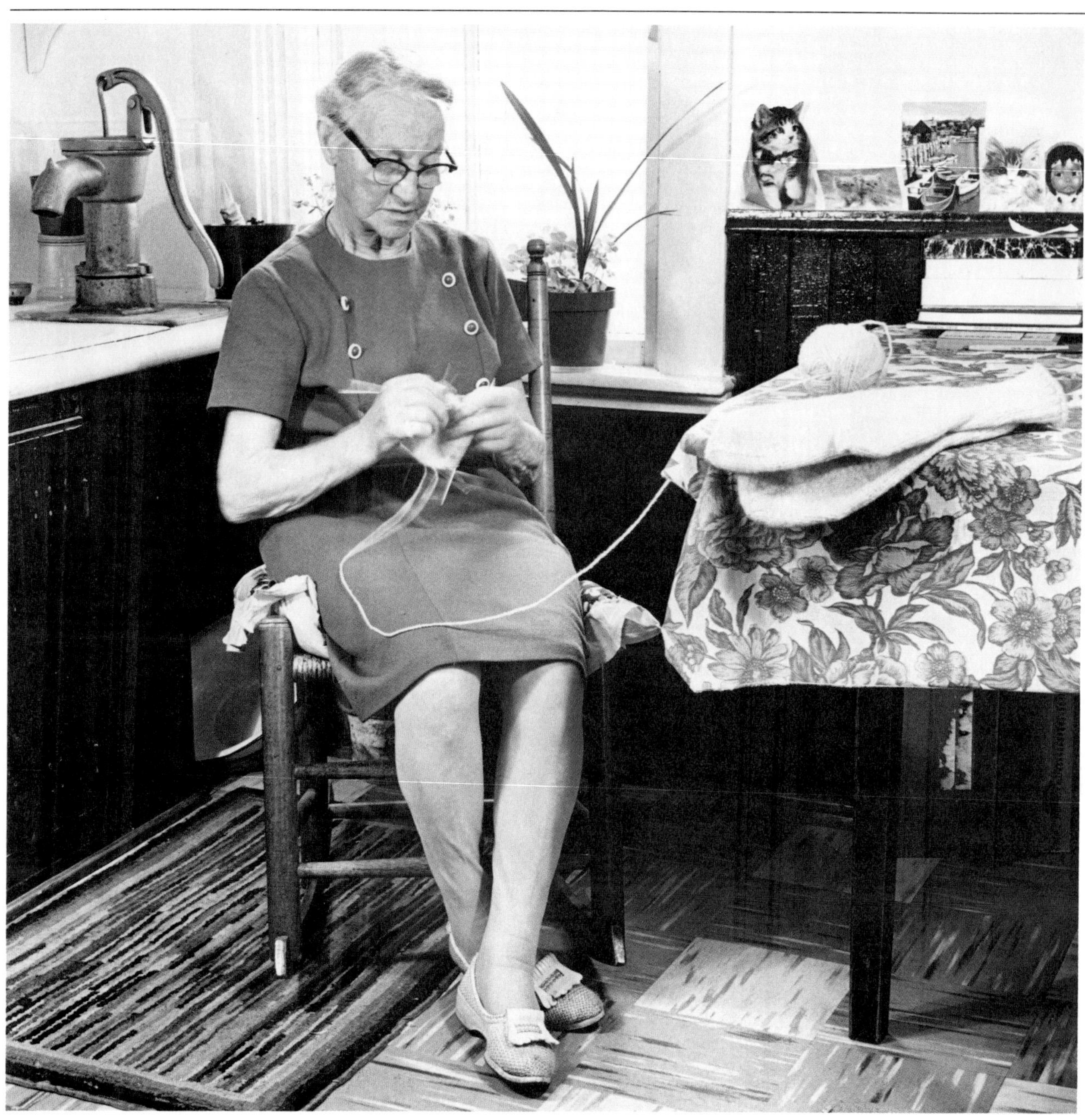

Eva Young

Born 8 November 1896, Lobster Mitts

All the fishermen around here used these mitts for lobsterin'. They were always knit large so they would shrink in the salt water, shrink up tight an' keep their hands warm. That was cold work in the winter. I guess I worried about the men. Sometimes they wouldn't come in until all hours of the night. Years ago, they had rowboats – when I come here first they would take as much as three hundred traps in one day. Spend all day at it. Come in at one o'clock for dinner, an' then go out an' haul 'em until night. The mitts, I guess, helped some with the cold.

I began to knit when I was seven years old. Years ago, on a long winter evening, I used to make one mitten in a night, but I can't make my fingers fly any more. I had to give it up this spring . . . too much arthritis . . . but I had my garden. The pain is gone now. . . so I'll pick up my knittin' again. I've always liked to knit. I don't know what I'd do if I didn't have my knittin'.

There's many people growin' up today that don't think at all about "sittin' down work" as I call it. That's true – off somewhere to a show at one place or another, and television. Things are too easy today. I wouldn't know if it's a good change or a bad one. I think it's nice if someone picks up something to use their time, don't you?

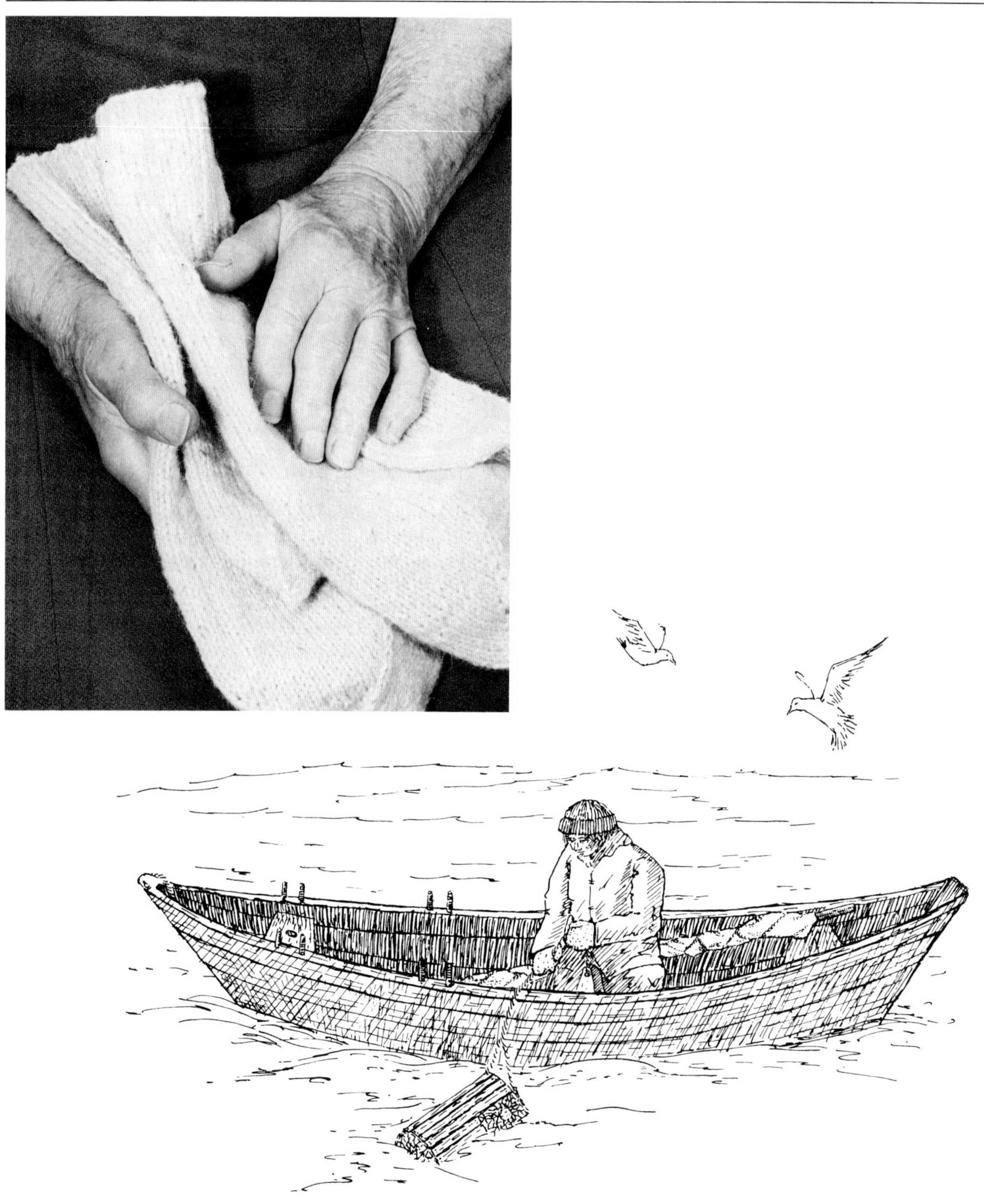

When the fishermen tend their traps during the lobster season, they need protection from the icy cold Atlantic waters. Although insulated rubber gloves are now available in most hardware stores, some men prefer to wear the old-style hand-knitted mitts made by their womenfolk.

The mitts are knit very big and as the men work in the cold salt water baiting and setting the traps, the wool shrinks and mats making them thick and practically waterproof. Only the naturally coloured white wool is used to knit these mitts, for it is generally believed by the fishermen that grey mitts on a boat bring bad luck. In some areas, such as on Ironbound Island near the mouth of Mahone Bay, where a group of men work together, the women crochet the man's first initial with coloured yarn on the mitt cuff to identify the owner.

Characteristic of her generation, Eva Young learned to knit when quite young. She knits her mittens on a round of five needles. The thumb and hand decreases are made in a spiral pattern and she does not graft off their ends; they are knit to a point.

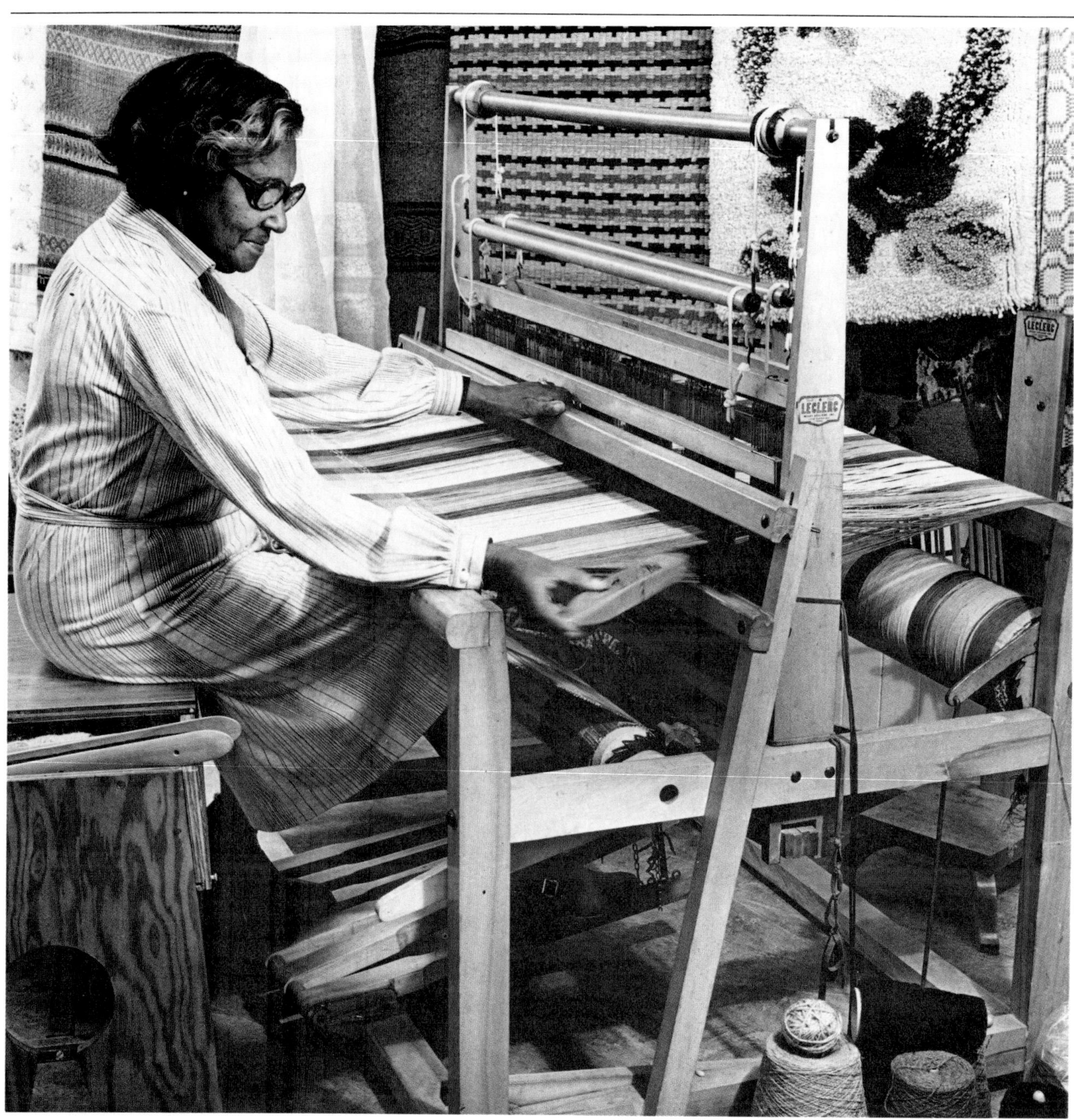
LECLERC
LECLERC

Peryle Lowe

Born 31 May 1907, Weaver

Well, years ago, there were no places to buy ready-made articles. People grew their own flax and spun their own linen, spun their own yarns from wool gathered from their sheep. And they wove the material for their clothing, their blankets . . . for all their needs. When they sat down in the evening at the end of a day they could see what they had done, and it meant something to them! In those days they had to weave. Nearly every home had a loom – the looms were bigger then and usually one room was set aside just for the loom. In those days they made their own looms – built their own looms. And do you know what happened to those looms? A lot of people have said when they moved into homes, the old looms were in the attic or the cellar, and they cut them up for firewood because they didn't realize . . . it's too bad . . . but they didn't realize they were any good.

But weaving is one of the older things being revived now. I started by taking classes. And to tell you the truth, I took it just for the sake of taking it – to make things for the house and the children. And after I made a couple of articles, why someone saw them and they wanted them and so I just kept on. That was thirty years ago.

Working with my hands gives me the greatest satisfaction in the world. Weaving gives me the feeling of creation. Quite often I make up original designs working with different colours and textures. It sort of . . . well it keeps your mind active as well as . . . you put your whole self into it. Weaving is my first love and I try to . . . I'm a perfectionist. Not that anyone can be perfect . . . but I try to be. I try to do the very best I can. I take pride in

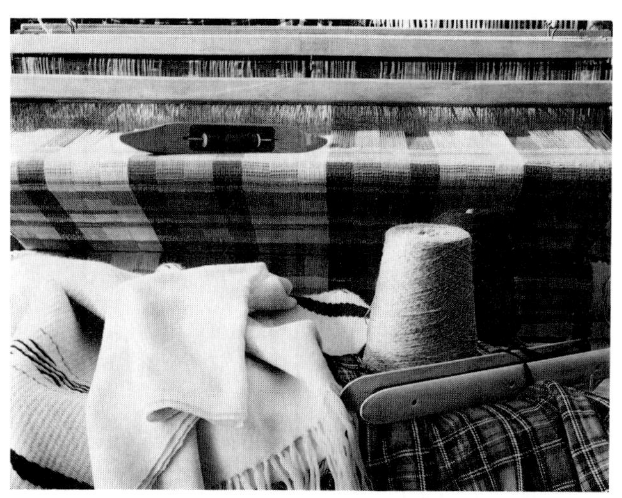

my work, because I feel that other people like . . . you know, they will love it as well. If I'm going to let them have something, I want it to be something I am proud of. I do some teaching and I always try to instill that feeling in my students.

It's nice that the young people are interested in carrying on an old tradition. It's too bad when it's not carried on . . . you know, when the family tradition is not carried on. I taught my daughter how to weave. She was interested as a small girl growing up, but then she went into the nursing profession. But after a number of years, she finally decided to give it all up and come back home and weave for which I was very, very happy. Now I know what's going to happen to my looms when I'm gone . . . not only my looms but . . . part of me. She made me very happy.

According to Harold and Dorothy Burnham in their study *Keep Me Warm One Night*, textile weaving came to Nova Scotia with French and Scottish settlers in the seventeenth and eighteenth centuries. A few sheep were brought to the province at that time, but the production of sufficient fleece for spinning yarn to supply the looms was a slow process. Many of the settlers grew hemp and flax which they processed into hemp and linen yarn. In weaving, two yarns were often combined. When weaving the long-wearing and warm "linsey-woolsey" cloth, for example, linen was used for the warp and wool for the weft. Later on, when the cotton industry became established in the southern United States, cotton was imported, replacing linen as the warp thread in blankets, sheeting and lightweight yardage.

Until very recently, weavers of Scottish descent in the isolated highlands of Cape Breton had been weaving woollen overshot coverlets for bed coverings using "drafts," patterns which had been handed down from one generation to another. Because of the narrow width of the loom, coverlets were always made in two pieces with a centre seam, and the pattern had to be matched along this seam. Many of these old coverlet drafts had charming names: The Rose in the Bush, True Love's Vine and Keep Me Warm One Night. Their heritage has been preserved in *Handweaving in Cape Breton* by M. Florence Mackley.

Tools for the production of yarn and cloth were also made in Nova Scotia – reels and clock reels, swifts, niddy-noddys, hackles, scutching knives, bobbin winders, shuttles and spinning wheels. Looms made in the province were of two types: the simple two-harness counterbalance kind for weaving tabby blankets, and the more complicated four-harness loom for weaving twill yardage and overshot coverlets. Weaving is a strong, living craft in Nova Scotia, and many of these spinning and weaving tools are still in use today.

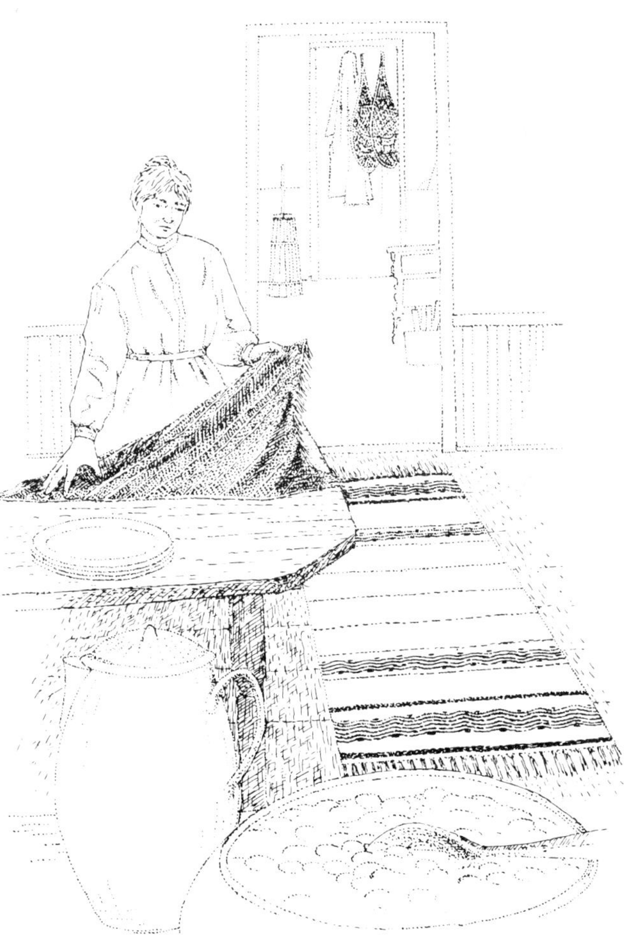

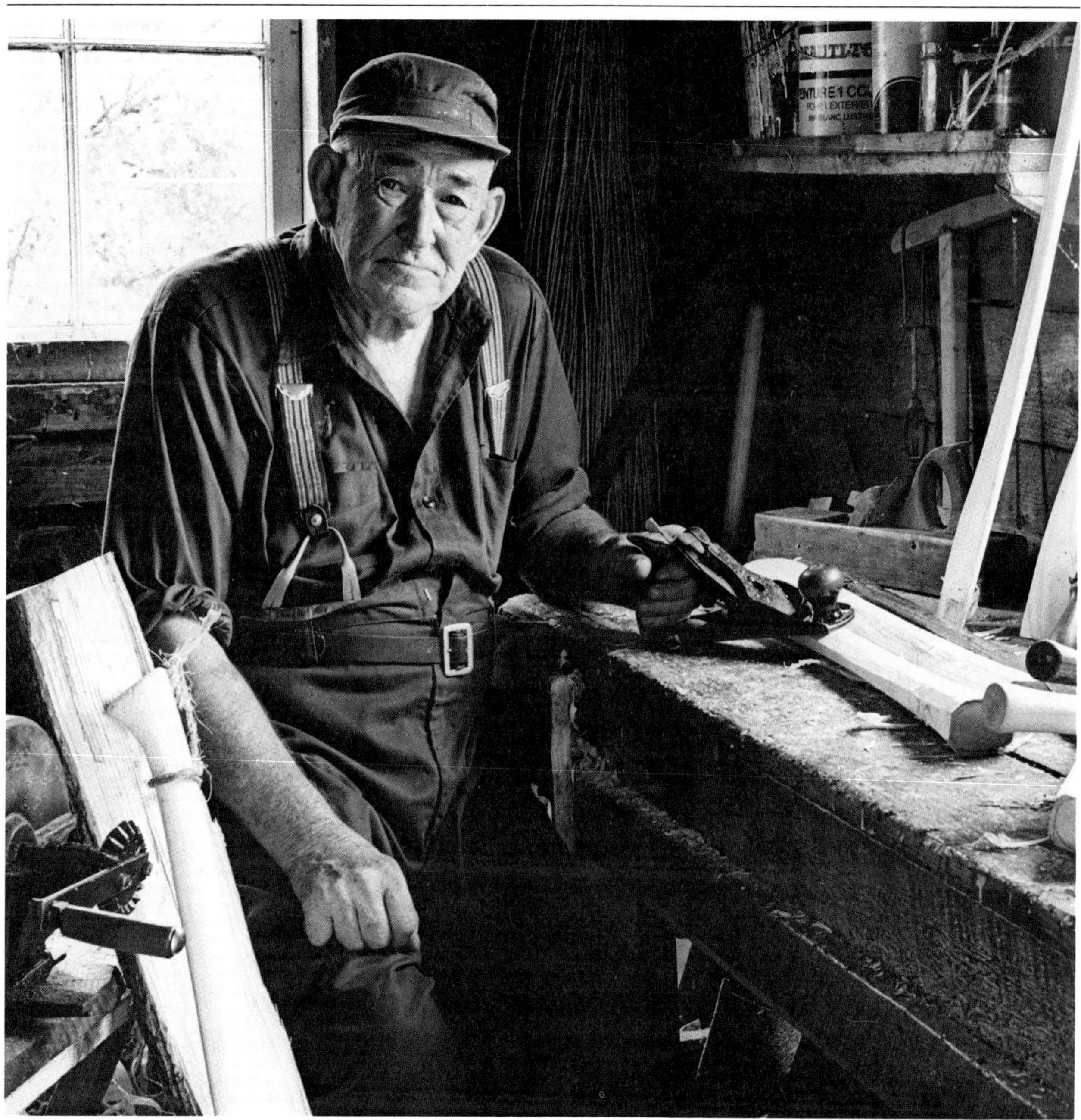

David Wile

Born 22 September 1897, Tool Handles

Grew up on a farm. My father went blind an' sick. When I was twelve years old, he took me out of school an' I was put to work . . . on the place drivin' the old horse. That summer I was twelve years old – they used to mow with a one horse mowin' machine. Sent me on the mowin' machine. "Now you do the mowin' this summer." Well I was as big as any of 'em an' pretty strong. No reason why I couldn't work. At them times, when a boy was pretty well growed up, he went to work. An' there was no foolin' about it!

An' in what spare time I had, I was always chippin' at somethin'. That's how I come to make these handles . . . made all the handles we used on the farm. Them times a farmer worked in mostly hand work . . . lots o' hand tools. I was chippin', tryin' to make somethin' all my life . . . from the time I was big enough to run around. It was a habit with me more than anything else. You learn things . . . you look for the best way to do it. You pick up things as you go along, workin' at it. As long as I could chip at somethin', I was satisfied. I remember one time I was workin' at a piece o' wood an' I was cuttin' an' cuttin' – cut my thumb pretty well off. Yes! I didn't cut the bone – just the most of it. After that I learned to keep my fingers off the end of the wood. Well, you don't forget it when you learn the hard way! You don't forget it.

A lot o' people could make handles as well as I could, but they don't try to do it. A feller over here, well he went an' bought a couple handles from me a year or two ago. Paid me for 'em. An' he was a carpenter! Had a big chest full o' tools. Now what was them tools for?

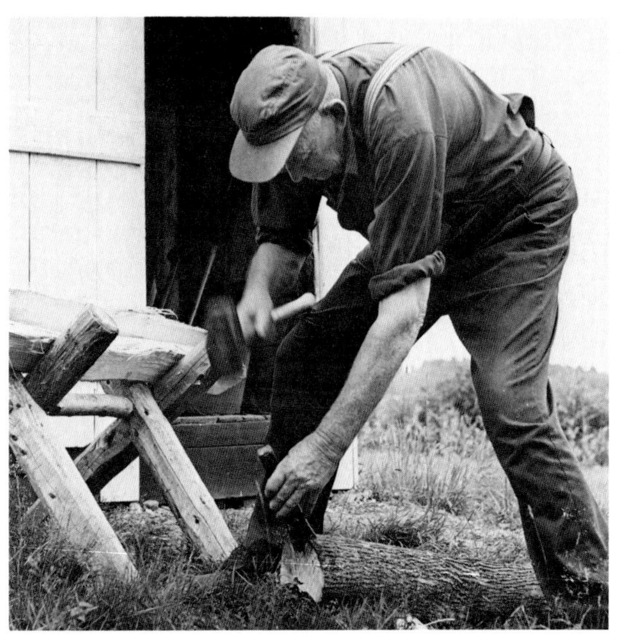

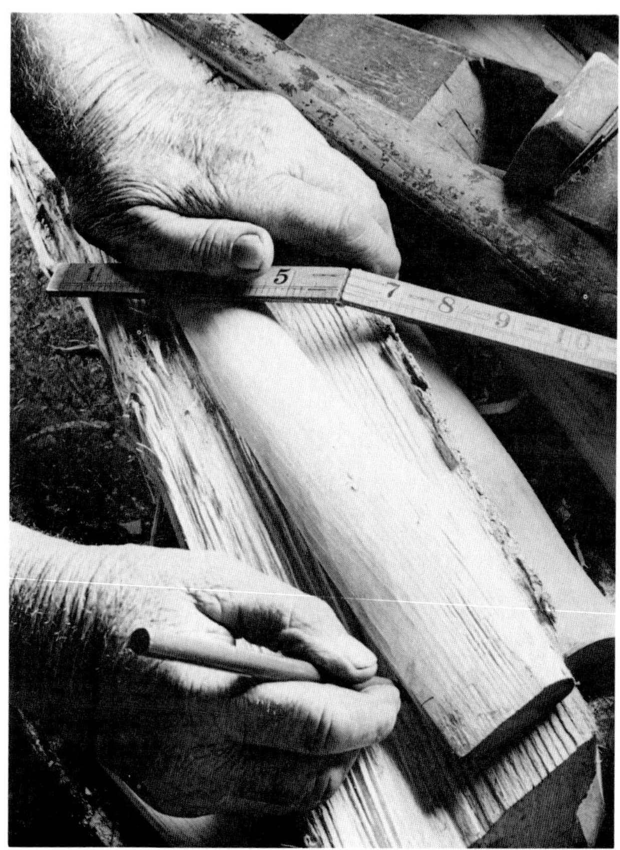

Handle-making is a country craft which is as highly regarded today as it was in times past. Well-made handles reveal a certain reverence for both the raw material and the purpose for which they are intended.

David Wile makes handles for hammers, hoes, axes and other farm and garden tools: "I always make handles out of wood that will suit them to it. If you can get a piece of wood with the grain running the length of the shape of the handle, straight grain the whole way, it makes a tougher handle...but you can't always fit it." He does not make his handles straight and round, for he finds, "...if they was straight, they's apt to roll, an' you would find it hard to keep a grip on your handle, you know, to keep a hoe from rollin'."

David uses only dry wood: "If you make 'em out of dry wood, they'll stay the way you make 'em. Make 'em out of green wood, they may dry too fast, twist a little, and they shrink a lot." White ash is preferred, presumably for its strength and hardness: "Lotta these old swamps has what we call 'yellow ash'; it's no good for handles–brittle and splinters. White ash that grows up on high ground makes the best wood for handles."

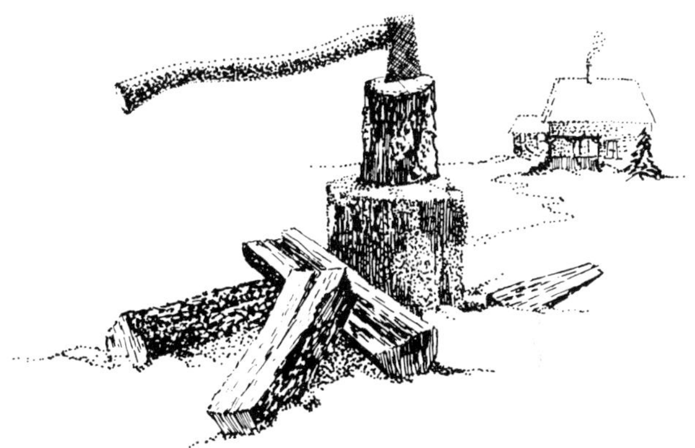

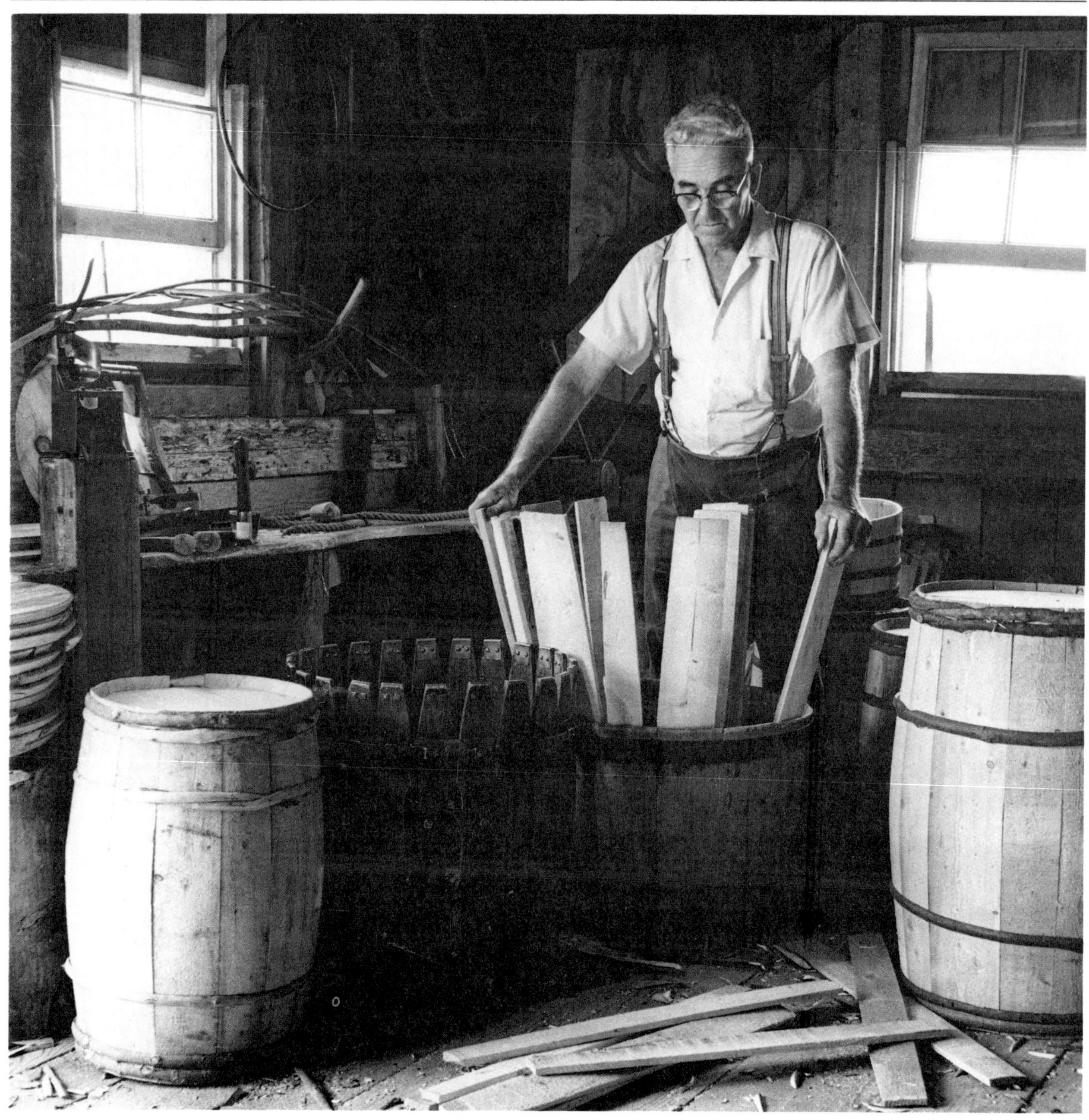

Ray Gates

Born 6 September 1911, Cooper

Until 1863, they made all fish barrels here – barrels that is watertight. An' sometime that year a feller was workin' in the Valley – he knew they made fish barrels here – he came out for apple barrels. An apple barrel is what they call dry barrels – they don't hold wet. Fifty of 'em was made, and this feller took 'em up to the Valley an' sold 'em for fifty cents apiece. An' different ones started makin' 'em – a feller by the name of Meister, he started makin' 'em in 1864. It just kept goin' on that way, more an' more. It got to be a big business – a good crop of apples, we used to have around two million barrels in the Annapolis Valley, I guess. Everybody, pretty near, around these parts made barrels. My father, see, he had a little farm, an' he'd plant his crop an' then, between the plantin' an' the hayin', he'd make some barrels. An' after he'd make his hay, an' then between the hay an' the harvest, he'd make some more barrels. Now some places'd have four or five men – they'd be full-time all summer, from June say to October, November. When the apples were picked, they were done makin' barrels – for that year.

As I was sayin', my father was a cooper, an' my grandfather before him. So I'm like the third generation makin' barrels. When I first started to set up barrels, I don't think I was over probably ten or twelve years old. I was right young . . . I used to go in my father's shop after school an' set up barrels. After I could do that pretty good, I forged 'em. Well, time went on . . . why I put the hoops onto them. Those are the three steps of makin' a barrel . . . raisin' 'em, forgin' 'em, an' hoopin' 'em. I don't think I was over fifteen or so when I could make a barrel right out an' out.

Worked along with my father like that. Dad, he made barrels all his lifetime, practically right up to . . . the day he was seventy years old he made forty-seven o' them fish drums. More than I can do now!

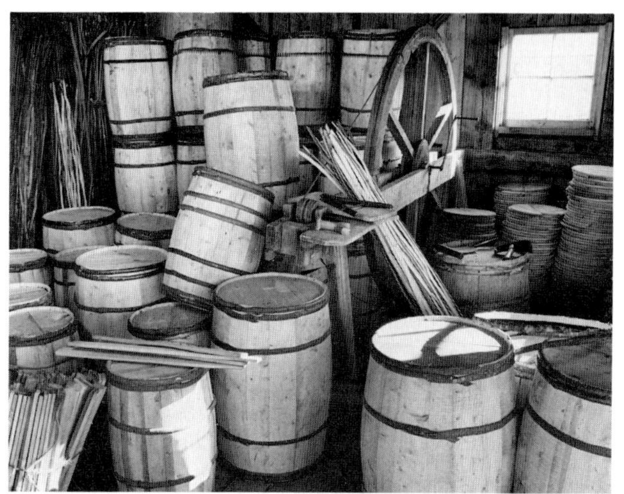

Today there'd be no point in a young feller to learn how to make barrels, 'cause they wouldn't have anything to do anyway. There's no call for apple barrels . . . everything changes. They tell me for shipping – they used to ship 'em overseas, you know, England was our main market – an' they say on the boats they wanted square boxes. They pack better or somethin'. Them things like that – you take right around the stores, for instance, you couldn't sell a barrel of apples. They got to be all packaged . . . plastic bags now, of course. Makes me feel kind o' bad. I really enjoyed makin' barrels. It's hot work. Lost lots o' sweat! But I enjoyed it.

There was a time not so long ago when domestic goods, such as flour, sugar, apples, fish, molasses and liquor, were either shipped or stored in barrels. Many men coopered in addition to farming, lumbering or other work. They cut wood from their own lots, took it to the local sawmill to be sawn into boards and cut into staves with the stave saw and the jointer. The jointer was a long, five- or six-foot plane with a blade over which the staves were drawn to cut them so they were wider in the middle than they were on the ends; it gave "a little bow into 'em" or what coopers refer to as a "bilge."

The making of apple barrels was essentially a Lunenburg County enterprise, according to Reverend T. A. Meister in *The Apple Barrel Industry in Nova Scotia*. The links between this county and the apple-producing county of Kings have always been strong. As Ray Gates says, it was a Lunenburg County man, working in the Annapolis Valley, who solved the apple industry's shipping problems by suggesting to his cooper friends that they adapt their fish barrels to carry apples.

An apple barrel is called a "dry" barrel, because it is made for the shipping and storage of dry items. Fish and rain barrels are called "wet," because they are made to hold liquid. "They're both made on the same principle; the only thing is with the fish barrel, you have to be more particular, an' you have to have better wood, better staves, an' heads, an' everything."

Apple barrel staves are made mostly of spruce, fir or poplar. Some are made with birch, but this makes for a heavy barrel. The heads are made of pine, a wood not well suited for staves, because it is too soft and would break easily under pressure. The hoops are made from hardwood saplings, such as birch, maple or oak, which are cut in half lengthwise.

According to Ray Gates, to make a barrel, "The staves are first set in a tub, then put on the heater to heat... an' then taken over, put in the jack an' forged... an' then the hoops are put on. In all, there are three steps – raisin' 'em, forgin' 'em and hoopin' 'em."

In the late nineteenth century, when the barrel became the unit of purchase of apples, it was necessary to legally standardize its size. "Inspectors visited the cooper shops regularly to check on the size of the barrels, sixty-four-inch bilge, that was the law. The bilge is right around the centre of the barrel. The staves may be different widths, but they all got to have the same bilge onto 'em. You see, the jointers are set so, I think, the staves are nine-sixteenths of an inch wider in the middle than they are on the ends. The first thing the inspectors would do, is to go down to the mill and they'd set the jointers, so then all the staves would have the right bilge into 'em. Well then, the cooper had no excuse. The inspectors would allow a little, you know, half an inch, say sixty-three and a half or sixty-four and a half, but if there was one say, sixty-six or one sixty-two, why then, you're in trouble right there. An' your bilge hoop had to be so many inches from the top, I think it was seven inches. Then, they had a law that you had to stamp every barrel, put your name onto 'em. Oh yes, there was a law to go by."

With the changes in the apple industry, wooden dry barrels gave way to square cardboard boxes. The craft of dry barrel coopering remains alive today solely as a visitor attraction at the Ross Farm Agricultural Museum in Lunenburg County.

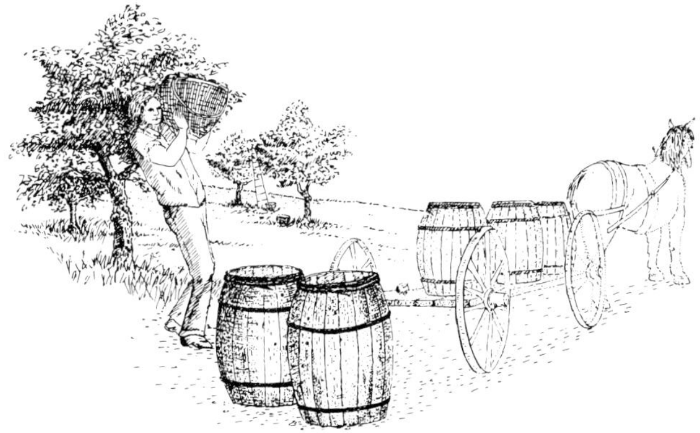

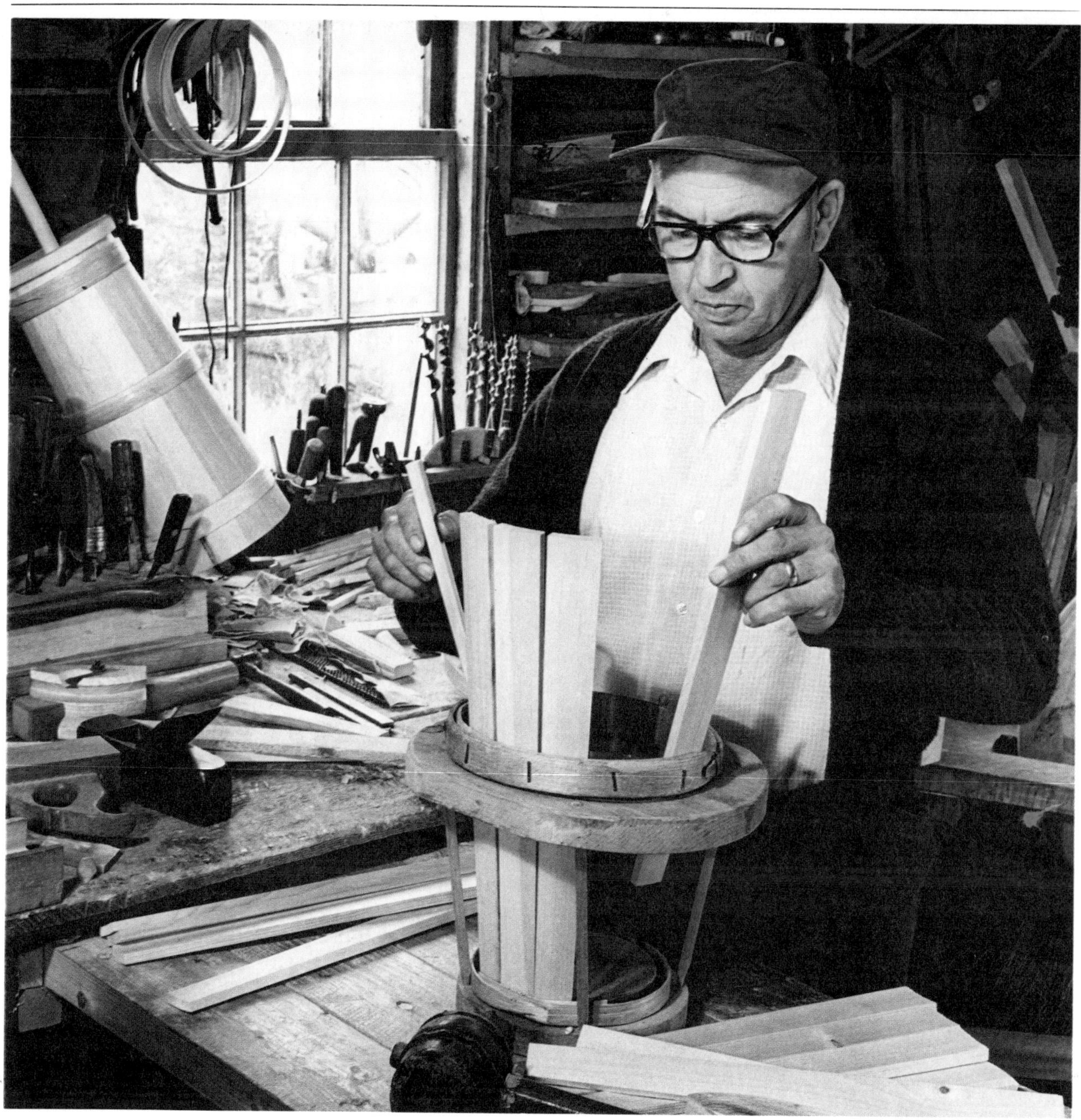

Ashton Reeves

Born 30 December 1925, Butter Churns

I would say every farm at one time had a churn. I don't think at that time you could buy factory butter or creamery butter. Most everyone had a cow, an' those that had a cow had a churn. Everybody made their own butter.

Now on the farm, we got up at six or half past, you know – you never laid in bed. Didn't want to 'cause you always used to go to bed at eight or half past – never stayed up late like today. If dad was away workin' in the woods through the winter months, why my mother, she used to build the fire or sometimes, if I got up first, well, I would build it. We'd have breakfast, then sit . . . whose ever turn it was would sit by the stove an' churn. Used to be good fun . . . especially in the winter. I can remember that you'd have to sit by the stove. If you didn't, why you'd freeze for awhile! Houses was cold in them days! Wood fire'd be out in the night. The first I remember churnin', I was eight. When dad was away, my brother an' I milked the cows an' saved the cream for churnin'. An' then every two or three days – just accordin' to the amount of cream that was got – we'd make the butter. My sister was the oldest, she'd take her turn, next time it would be my turn, an' next time it would be my brother's. That's the way we worked – the oldest first. That's how we'd get the butter started. At that time it always seemed to be good fun – jump up behind the churn for half an hour afore you left for school. Then mother would finish it – wash it an' salt it.

Made all our own butter – all for our own use – unless someone wanted a pound of butter an' you'd give it to them, just for to be neighbourly.

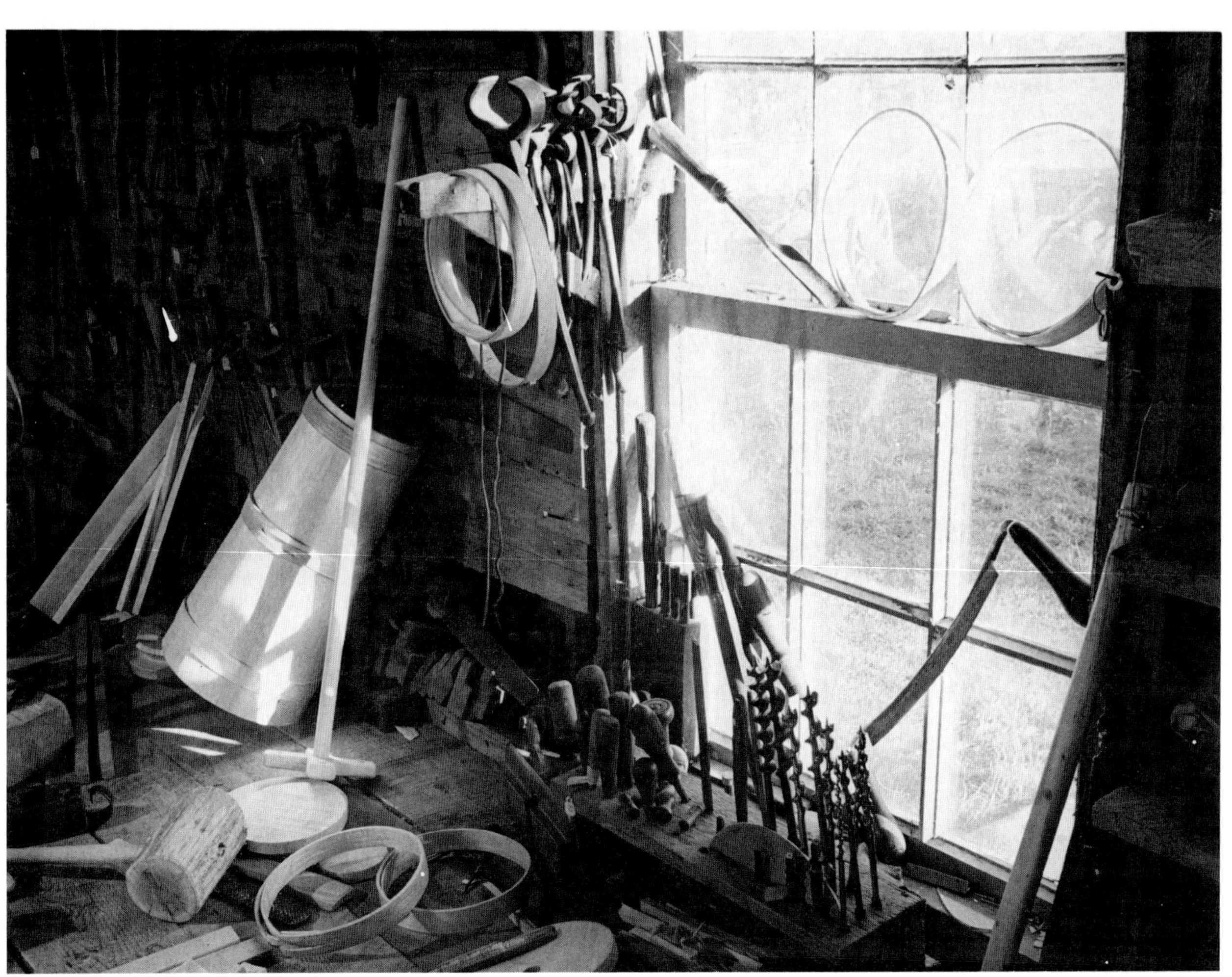

Butter churn making is a craft which has been revived in Nova Scotia to fit into the historic setting of the Ross Farm Agricultural Museum in Lunenburg County.

According to J. Lynton Martin, in *The Ross Farm Story*, the earliest churn was "...the plunger type made of either wood or earthenware." Other models were boxes or barrels on rockers which were manipulated by a foot pedal leaving the hands free for other work. Churning involved a great amount of work, so it is not surprising to find a number of "labour-saving" churn designs on the market in the middle of the nineteenth century.

The churns made by Ashton Reeves are small floor models. They are made like the barrels described by Ray Gates (page 69); the pine staves are cut, jointed, planed and set up in a stand in the same way, except the size of the stand is smaller. As Ashton explains, "After I get 'em all set up, drawed together, why I start hoopin' 'em. My hoops are made out of oak, I split 'em out with the froe, shave 'em down with the drawknife. I don't use nails; I use locks, an' I can't tell you the name of the lock, 'cause it's somethin' that I started myself. I thought I'd try to hold the hoop on that way an' it worked out fairly good...makes a churn good an' strong."

The bottom and top, each called a "head," are made of pine and fit into grooves cut into the staves. The top head has a centre hole through which the dasher slides: "My dash handle, I make out of inch-square board, an' I shave it out with the plane. The dash is made out of two pieces fitted together, an' I cut the centre out of it, an' I fit in the handle...use a little sandpaper to finish it smooth."

For those who might be interested in pursuing the early craft of butter churning, it is described in *A Guide to Some Domestic Pioneer Skills*, by Mary Sparling.

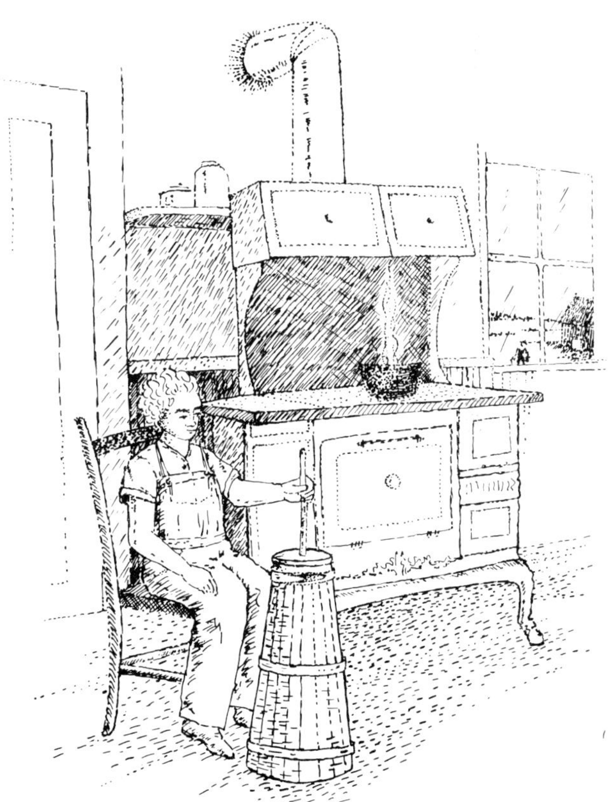

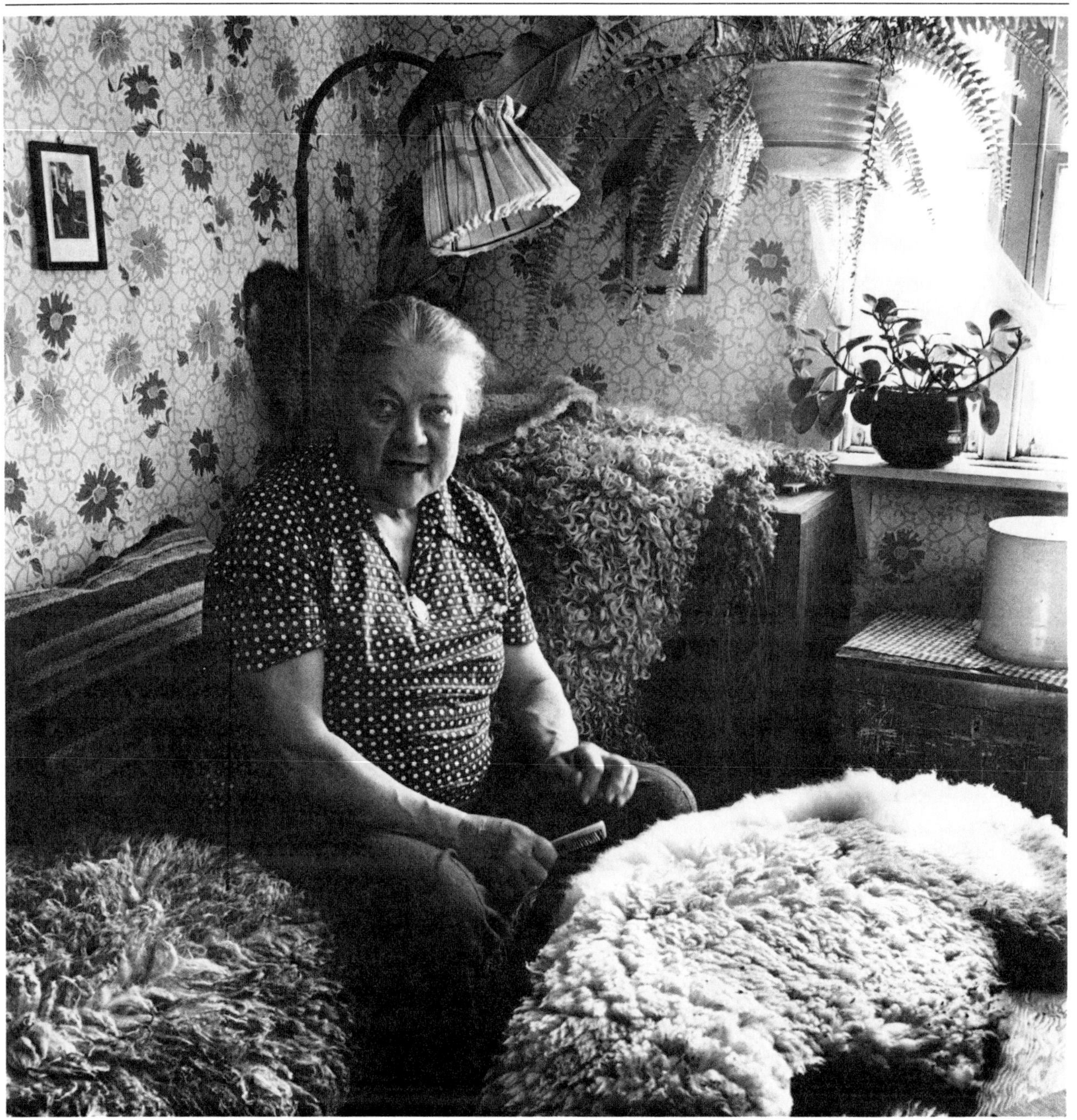

Edith Zillig

Born 4 August 1915, Sheepskin Tanner

When we first had our own sheep here, we sold the hides to a hide dealer. He had a man in the village who gathered cow and calf hides and sheepskins. And once a month, that man came with a big truck and took all the hides and paid you. If it was a hide like this with so much wool and so large, he gave you fifty or sixty cents. And for the little Easter lambskins, he said, "Throw them on the manure pile. It's not worthwhile for me to bother." I thought that that was a shame. That hide dealer, he didn't care for the leather. He took the wool off – put it in some solution that took the wool off – and sold the wool to a wool mill.

I thought if I tan it and I make a nice product out of it, it is not a waste. A farmer doesn't make much money, so he should put everything he can to some use. When I started with it years ago, I did maybe three or four a year. People saw the hides drying outside and asked if I would do some for them for winter – for Christmas presents. One year I tanned twenty-eight hides. I remember I was so proud. Twenty-eight was a big amount for me at that time. Then I increased it to forty-five, and I thought that was quite a bit. But over the years . . . I tan all the hides from the sheep we butcher. Nothing goes to waste.

I think that every sheep-farmer's wife could do it at home. I have quite a lot of people who want to learn it from me. And I explain it and show it to them. When I meet these people one or two years later, I ask them, "How did you make out?"

"Oh," they say, "I did one or two . . . yes, they came out nice. But really, it's a little bit too much work involved." I really feel sorry for them. Look, you can't expect even the

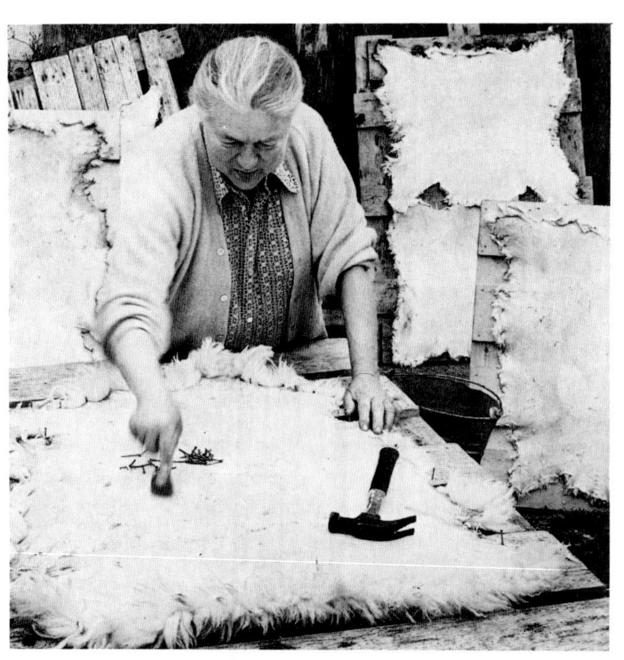

minimum wage – you will never get that. Maybe if I make twenty-five cents an hour – I'm completely happy with that. First, the hide is used and otherwise it is wasted. On the other hand, if I would have a job in town, I would leave in the morning, be away all day... who should look after the farm animals, my household and my family? Maybe I'm old-fashioned?

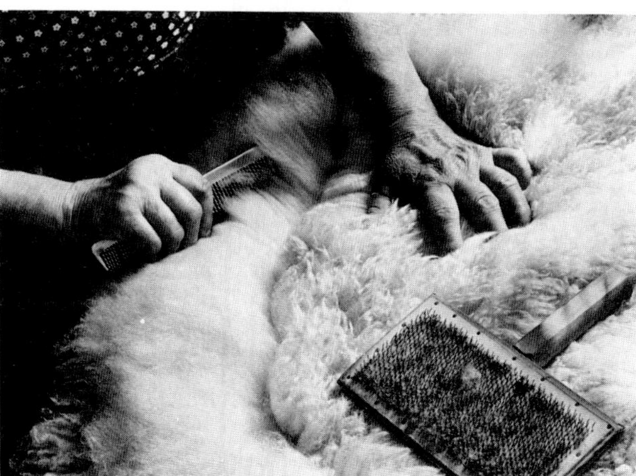

Edith Zillig has two methods of preserving her sheepskins. The first uses alum and salt, referred to as "tawing" in the past. After washing, the skins are soaked for two days in a solution of equal parts of alum and salt, stretched to dry on wooden frames, the flesh side is scraped (curried) and the fleece is combed with a wool carder. The alum makes the skin contract, giving the finished pelt a lovely thick pile. These skins cannot be exposed to moisture, because they are only preserved, not tanned, and so they are used as chair and floor mats.

The second method involves preserving the skins in a "pickle bath" for a few days and then tanning them in a mixture of salt and chrome. After drying, scraping and combing, the skin is soft, pliable and suitable for making garments.

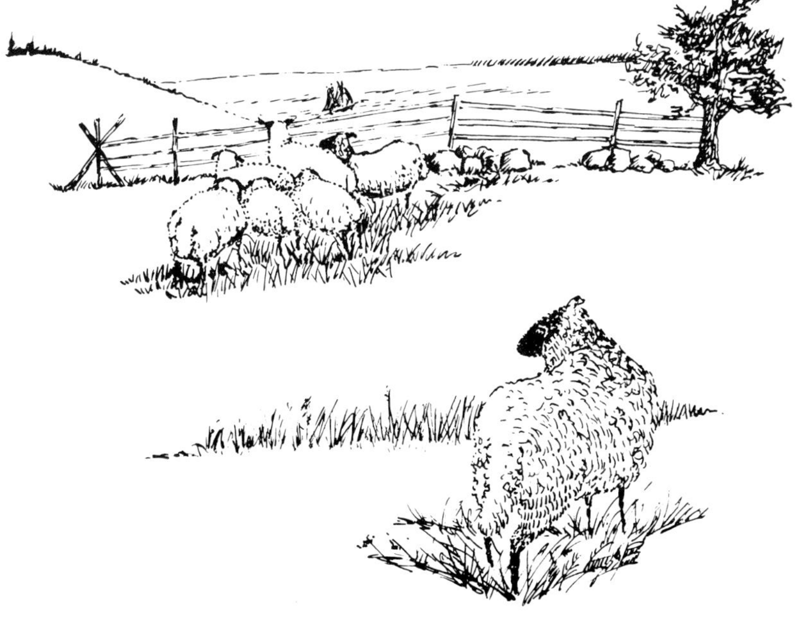

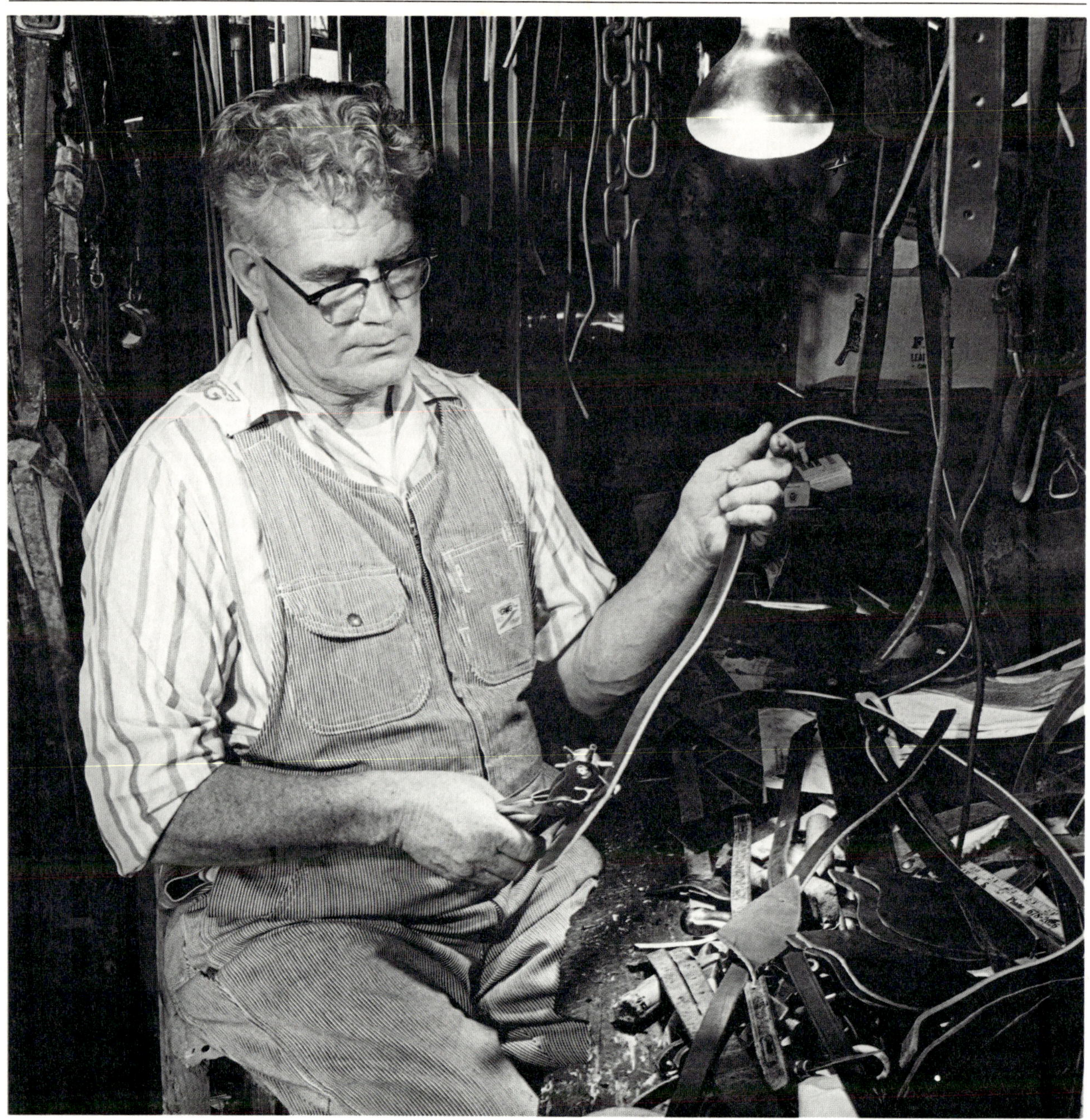

Bernard Young

Born 14 January 1918, Harness-Maker

I was interested in horses . . . we always had a horse an' I just got interested. Always had it in my mind to handle horses on my own. I always did. An' this is how the whole thing came about. I learned harness-makin' on my own. I kept pickin' it up.

Years ago, every town had at least two, three harness-makers. They needed 'em. Horses was used for ploughin', harrowin', hayin'–you name it. Everythin' was done by horses at that time. Most every farmer had, well, I'd say, on the average, they'd have a pair o' work horses–the smaller farmers–then, they'd have a drivin' horse. Some farmers had as high as three or four teams. They'd need a harness for each team. Right straight through the Valley there was harness shops in every town. An' now I'm the only one around, but there is a future in this. I think in this day an' age of high energy cost that somethin' is really goin' to take place–usin' horses on the farm is goin' to be on the increase.

Anyways, I learned from them older fellers. I was interested. I was very interested. I picked it up mostly by goin' in the shops . . . talkin' to 'em, so on an' so forth. Came back to my shop . . . kept buildin' up. Kept doin' it that way. You can learn so simple sometimes by just watchin' somebody else or comin' across some old guy that's been doin' this for years. An' you're never too old to learn. There's often times I'll sit here an' I'll think about, well . . . I'd like to make some kind o' design for somethin' on a horse–then, maybe I'll get my knife an' a piece o' leather an' I'll go at it. Puzzle it out, see. First thing I'll come up with somethin'. Even today with that many years I've been at it, I can still learn.

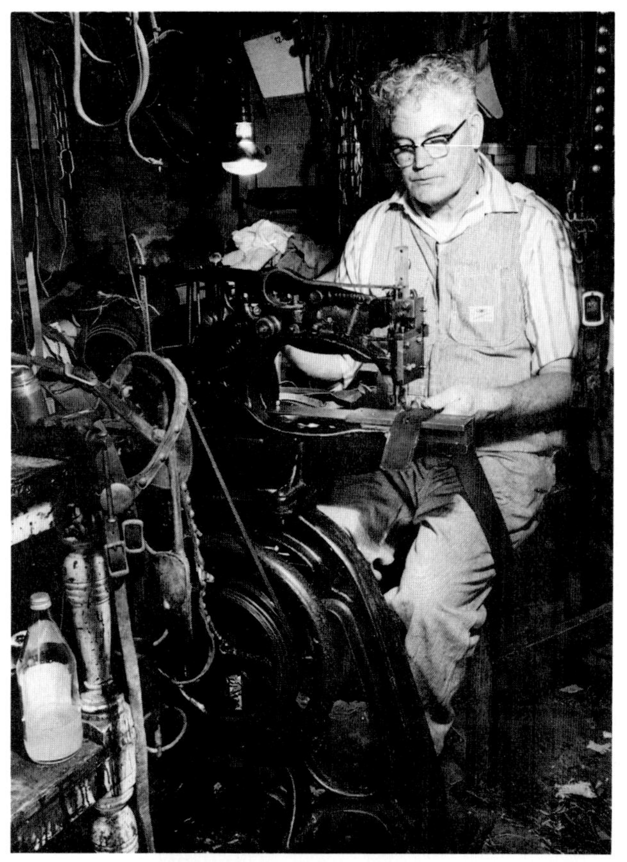

I consider when I'm makin' somethin' . . . for instance, you come in here an' you order somethin' . . . I'm just as fussy about that an' just worry about whether it's goin' to suit you as it would myself. An' I figure if it suits me, it's goin' to suit somebody else. I really want it to.

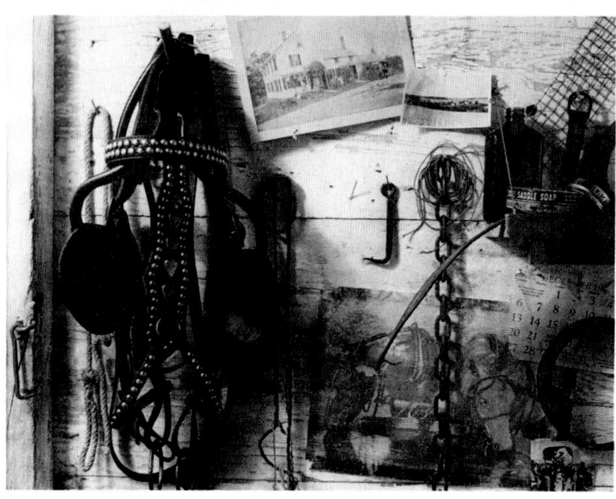

Although most of the saddlery used today in Nova Scotia is imported from England, Argentina and Germany, there are still a few harness-makers working in the province. Technically, "harness" is a comprehensive term used for the bridle, collar, pad, reins, etc., used for the driven horse. There are various types of harness for various vehicles.

As Bernard Young says, "The quality of the leather is the main thing in a harness... the quality of the leather, an' that can be told by the fibre in your leather. Western hides are much heavier, better grade, than our local hides, because they're wintered out in the cold, where ours are mostly in the barn. So, you get a thicker hide an' a much better type of leather than you would on our own steers." The quality of leather determines whether it will be used for making blinkers, where there is no strain on it, or whether it will be used for traces or girth straps, which receive a lot of strain from both the horse and the rider. A girth strap made of inferior leather will soon stretch and become useless.

Bernard makes both heavy and fine harness. Heavy harness for the workhorses is made of a good, strong leather; the fine harness for show animals is made of a lighter leather with neater and finer cutting and stitching. He decorates his harness with brasses of various shapes. These horse brasses, or amulets, have an interesting historical background. They were thought to have been first worn by camels in the desert as tokens to ward off the "evil eye" – the chances and dangers of the road. The Crusaders introduced them into Europe. There are a great number of different designs, many of which are based on the sun, moon and stars.

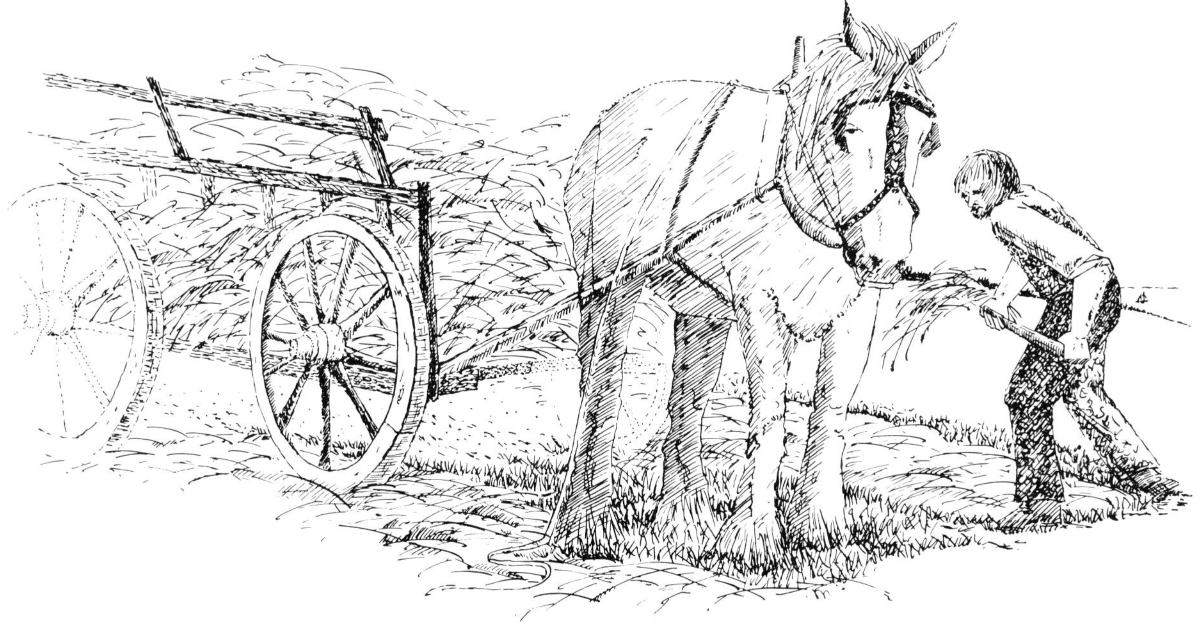

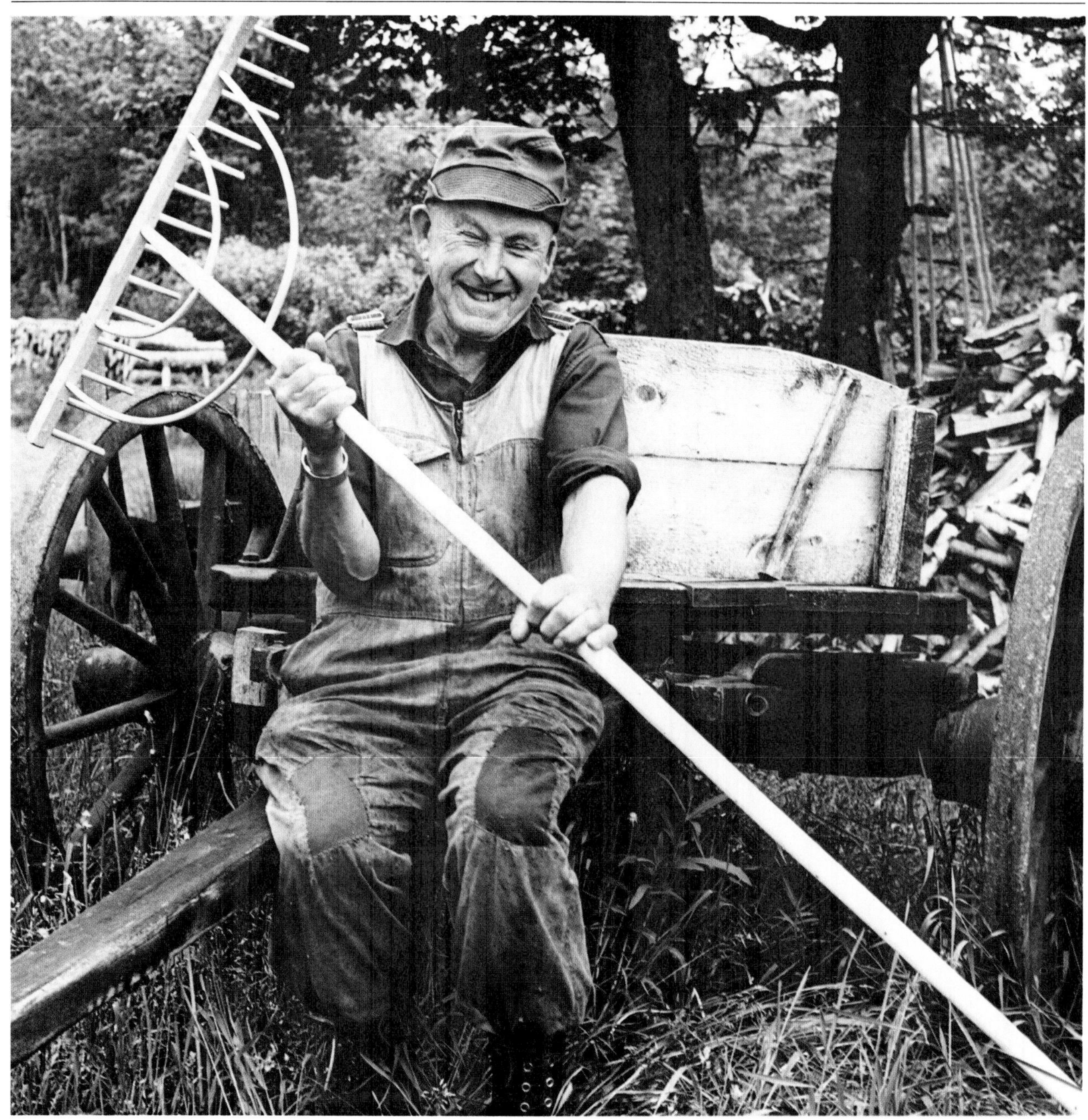

Sam Herman

Born 2 February 1903, Hayrakes

Store-bought rakes – them goddam things! Them things! They got the turned handles. They don't last because . . . turned handles, you see, are all cross-grained. An' the head is straight on 'em an' the teeth is set straight down so when you go to rake – pull hard – they break off. No good. That's all them hardware stores sell. I wouldn't mix mine among 'em. So much junk that's no good. I wouldn't bother with 'em. I wouldn't have 'em around! Them rakes that are made in a factory are no good.

I learnt to make rakes a long while ago in my young days. I seen my uncle make 'em when I was a kid. I was pretty sharp and, boys, I didn't say nothin' to nobody. I thought to myself, "I'm going' to try that." An' I did, an' I done it. Wasn't as good as them I make now – first one I done. But the more I make, the better I get. Learnt it out of my own head, how to make 'em. More I made, the more I seen how to do it. You learn things as you come along in the world – you work along, you learn by yourself. That's the best kind of learnin' you can get. Do it yourself. I found that out. You learn somethin' the hard way, that's the best thing you can do. That's why I can make 'em – made a lot of 'em.

By God, at one time that's all we had to rake hay with. No rakin' machines around at that time. Three or four of us – sometimes the whole family would go out an' rake up a big piece o' hay field. Rake it up in windrows – that's what we called 'em – windrows. By God we'd clean up a lot o' hay with hand rakes. We thought nothin' of it at one time. If people had to go at it with hand rakes today, they'd go wild!

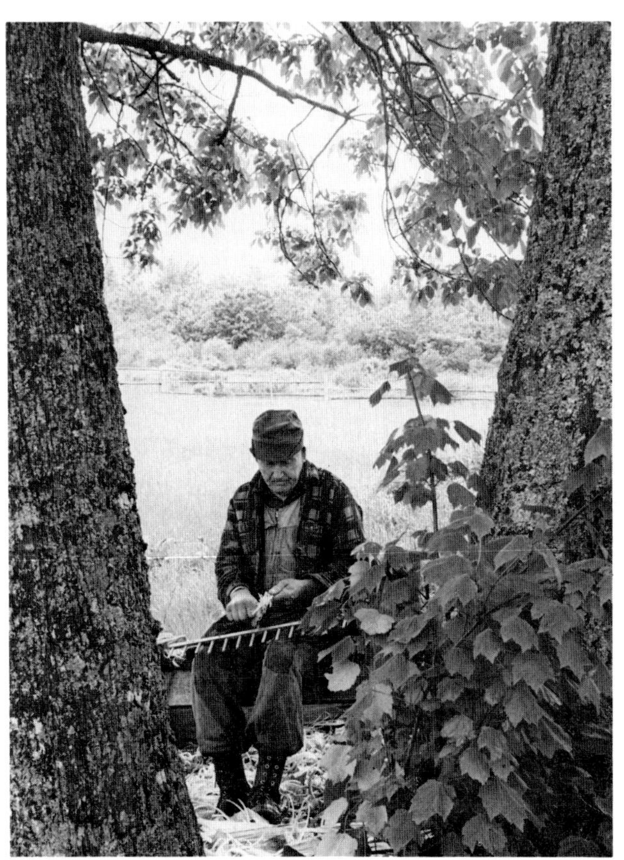

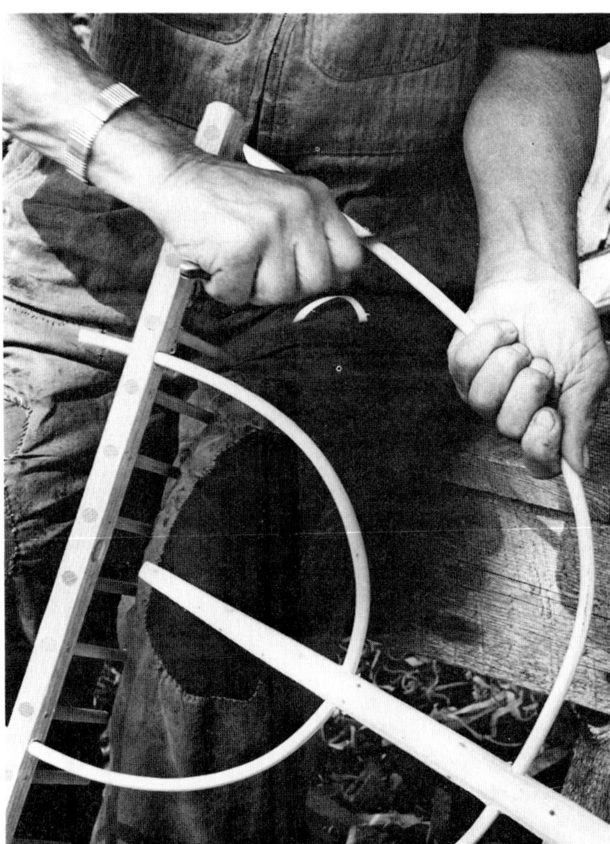

The design of the wooden hayrake has not changed appreciably over the past five centuries. Early fifteenth-century illuminated manuscripts, such as the famous *Duc de Berry's Book of Hours*, and woven wall hangings of the same period depict women using hayrakes which look very similar to those made in Lunenburg County today. A long handle fits into a rectangular head, set with sharpened wooden teeth, and the join between the head and the handle is strengthened by one or two pair of bowed pieces of wood.

Herbert L. Edlin, writing in *Woodland Crafts of Britain* (1949), described two types of hayrakes made in that country at that time. In the Midlands and in the south of England, the handle was split and inserted into the head in the shape of a Y. However, in the north and west, where a stronger rake was needed, the handle was not split but supported by one or two paired bows, similar to the rakes found in Lunenburg County.

In Nova Scotia, several different woods are used in the construction of the hayrake due to their different qualities of strength and pliability. Sam Herman uses "...ash for the heads, an' then ash for the teeth. They are all put together with little pins–them is ash too. The handle is spruce an' the bows is maple...the bows are made with green wood...shave 'em green, an' bend 'em up, an' tie 'em together, an' they stay that way...when they dry, they stay right there."

The teeth are set into the head on a slight angle, because the rakers find such a rake easier to use: "You don't have to drag so hard." The hay falls off easily, cleaning the rake after each sweep. Sam Herman determines the angle by an experienced eye: "I sight down, side of my head, an' bore my holes on up in there. Not often I get 'em crooked." If the teeth are set in straight, they present problems: "When they go to rake, they pull so hard, the teeth break off...they break much easier."

The teeth are held in place with small ash pins fitted into holes bored through the head and the top of the tooth. Sam does not like to use nails: "I don't like the idea of it, they're hard to get out sometimes. Once in awhile you will break a tooth, then you gotta take them pins out, knock out that piece of wood, put a new tooth in, an' pin it again...if it's a nail, sometimes it's hard, they're a son of a gun to get out, ya, so I don't put no nails in. No, I don't like 'em."

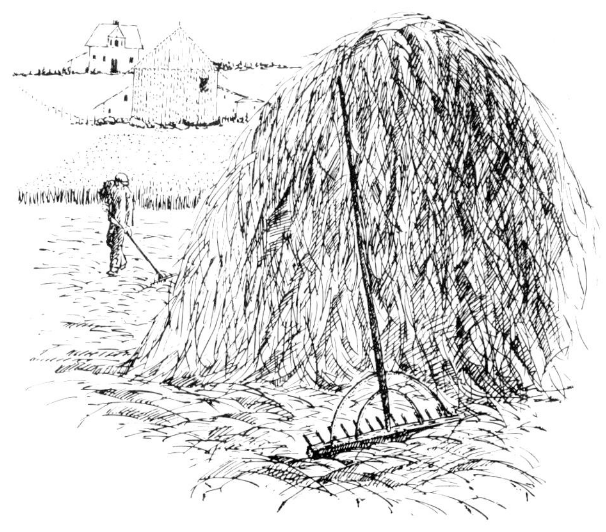

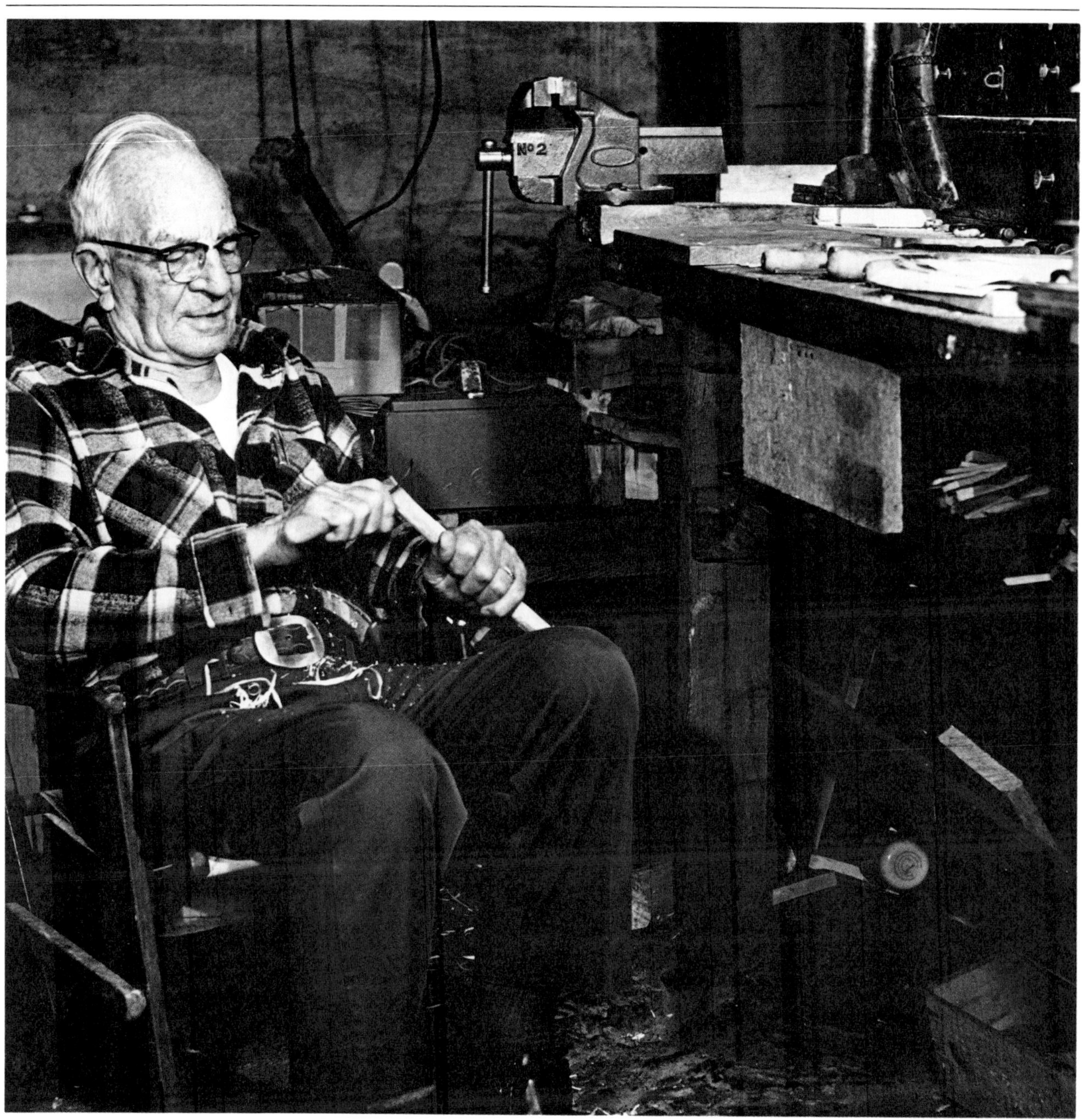
No2

Andrew Jackson Mooers

Born 7 May 1900, Crooked Knives

I used to go down here to the river when I was only a young lad, you know–school age. Used to go down there an' watch those old fellers dippin' kayaks only a little jump down here to the river. Indians. Most of 'em would be Indians. An' I used to go down there an' watch them. They'd be dippin' for these kayaks an' the salmon of course if they got one. Well, they wouldn't be allowed to start dippin' until twelve o'clock at noon. So they'd get there early, an' each had his place where he dipped. An' they'd sit there an' whittle these little pegs out with this crooked knife–each always had one. It was just a little peg only about an eighth of an inch in diameter I suppose. Then they had holes in this bow all the way around. An' they'd put the string across the hole an' drive this peg in to keep the net onto the bow–a wooden peg. An' that'd swell in there an' keep it tight. I used to watch them, you see . . . I used to watch 'em usin' it. An' then I asked one o' the old fellers. I said, "Can I have a look at your knife?" Showed me his knife and I watched him whittle with it.

He said, "You whittle with crooked knife?"

I said, "No . . . but by gosh I'm going to!"

So anyway, I come home an' told my father–he was a mechanic and carpenter, he was all 'round handy man an' he had three tool boxes full o' tools. An' we had an old workshop that was one end of the barn. An' I said, "Daddy, I'd like to have a crooked knife. I'd like to have one o' those crooked knives."

"Well," he said, "if you want a crooked knife, make one." I suppose I was ten, eleven years old. An' he said, "Make one." He give me a little

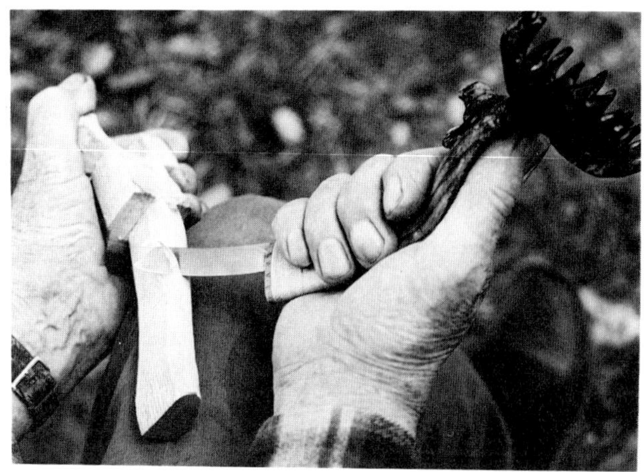

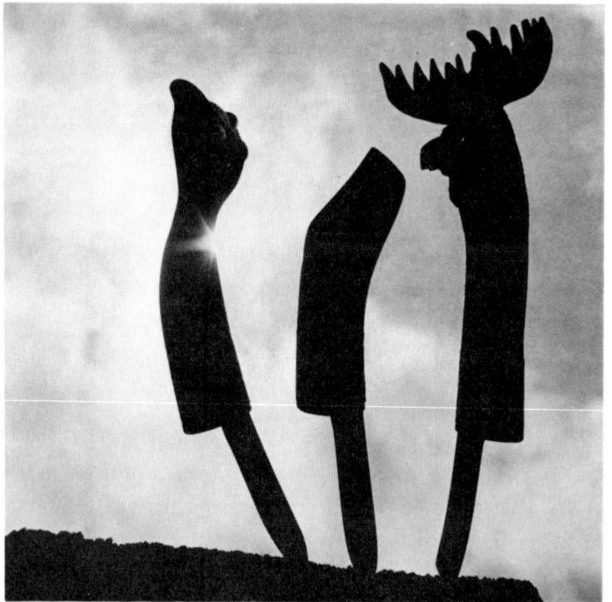

file, a flat file, an' he put it into the fire to draw a temper – then he gave me a good file. "Now," he said, "you go to work an' file yourself out a blade." So I filed an' I filed, I don't know, for days I guess – when I got a chance between other jobs, little jobs I had to do around the place. Finally, I got it down anyway an' then I got a chunk o' wood. I guess it was a piece o' pine. Then I made myself a handle. Well it was a queer lookin' thing! An' I put it in there an' I wound it all on there with string anyway, an' I had myself a crooked knife. And that was my first crooked knife!

I wish I knew how many I made since then. I can't tell you. I can't tell you. I just do it for something to do, that's all. Retired. It's just something I like to do. An' if I didn't have this workbench and all these tools. . . . I'll sit down here and I'll take a piece o' wood an' whittle out a handle. Maybe somebody'd come in here an' sit down an' talk awhile. Spend my time here. My, oh my, if I didn't have this place to come into, what would I do? I have to do something 'cause I've always worked with my hands. . . .

Many Nova Scotian woodsmen today use the traditional Micmac crooked knife. Prior to European contact, the Micmac Indians made a variety of knives with flaked or ground stone cutting edges. Because of the acidity of the soil in the Maritime Provinces, none of the wooden hafts for these knives have survived. However, some of them may have had handles of curved antler, much like the modern crooked knife.

When European adventurers and traders first came to North America, they brought with them metal blades to trade. At some later point, a type of knife very much like a farrier's tool (used to scrape out the frog of the horse's hoof prior to shoeing) was introduced. The blade had a curved tip and the handle had a curved shape. O.T. Mason, in *Aboriginal Indian Basketry*, notes that this tool was extremely popular as a trade item, perhaps due to its resemblance to pre-contact knives. Soon it became the main woodworking tool for the majority of North American Indians. Andy Mooers muses, "I've often wondered how many beaver skins and how much fur those old-timers gave the traders for one of those knives. Can't imagine, can you?"

For his knife blade, Andy might use a flat steel file, an old saw blade or an odd piece of steel. His blade has a slight curl and is set in at an angle to the main axis of the handle. The handles are made of a variety of woods, all having the traditional crook, and are often carved with elaborate figures. Micmac knives are bound with a variety of materials: sinew, spruce root, woodsplints and rabbit wire. Andy binds his handle and blade with heavy linen thread, which he covers with beeswax.

The crooked knife is characteristically held like a drawknife, with the cutting edge towards the carver. The handle is grasped with the palm of the hand under the handle, not over it, and the thumb fits in a depression carved into the outer end of the handle. The shape of the handle and the position of the hand gives the knife what Andy calls a "... purchase... you can cut so much deeper 'cause you got your thumb there pushin' against the handle."

After witnessing an accident to a friend with one of his knives, Andy has always made wooden sheaths for them. Each sheath is made out of two pieces of pine, hollowed out to fit that particular knife, glued together and covered with leather. As an Indian lady, old Mrs. Tom, said to him, "You got moxie... you use your head."

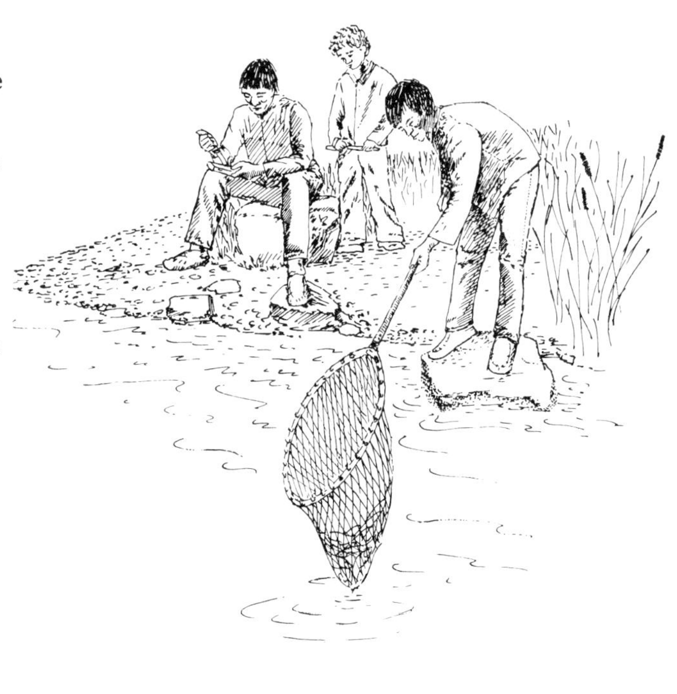

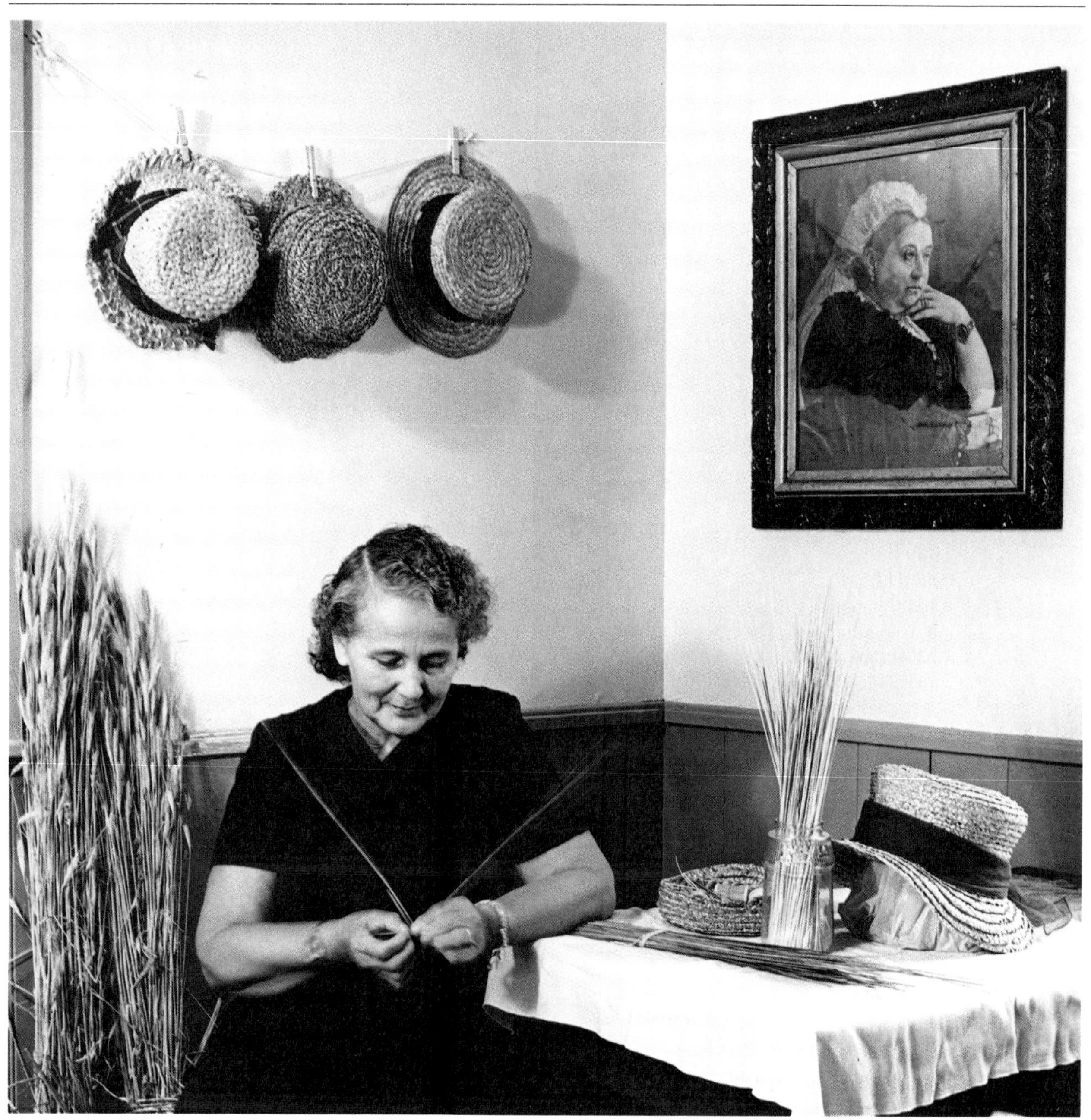

Jane Hiltz

Born 24 May 1914, Braided Hats

Braiding hats was the only means they had of making hats at home back in the 1800s. Years ago, father used to gather the grain, and him and the children used to prepare the straw. The children would do the braiding and the mother would sew the hat together . . . it was a family project. Wooden hats was what they used for their Sunday hats, where the straw and the rush was used more for gardening and out in the field. I heard the old people talk about it, and I always thought I'd like to learn. There was an old lady up here in Aldersville who made hats, and I said to her, "Mrs. Veinot, would you mind me comin' up one day and watching you so I could do it too?" She said she would be delighted. And she learned me how to do the braids. She learned me on thin strips of brown paper . . . learned the braids folding brown paper. She died in 1972 in the winter.

I started with the straw hats first. I grew my own oats, and then I prepared them and braided them and sewed them into a hat. And nothing goes to waste. You just use the top portion of the straw for the braid. The top seed is fed to the chickens and the rest is fed to the cattle or used for bedding in the barn. Now the rush you braid the same way as you do the straw, but when it dries, it dries out to more of a lacy effect, and that's why the rush hats look different than straw hats. With the wooden hats I got . . . I got my husband to go with me and cut a piece of yellow birch tree – three or four feet long. Peel the bark all off of it . . . into the white wood. Then you take a sharp knife and chip into your wood and then strip it . . . that's called a sheen and those sheens is what you braid to

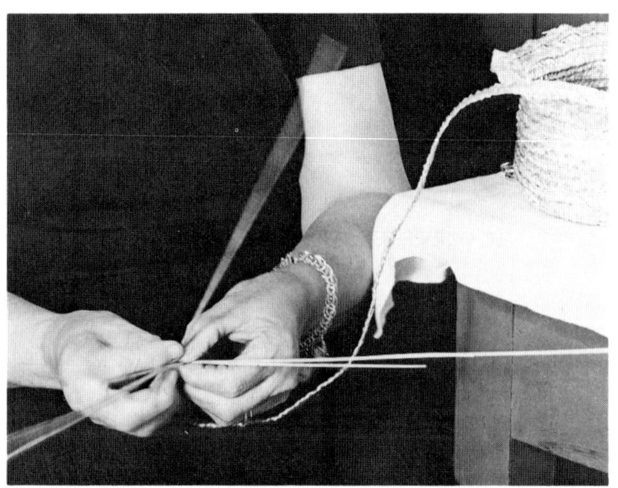

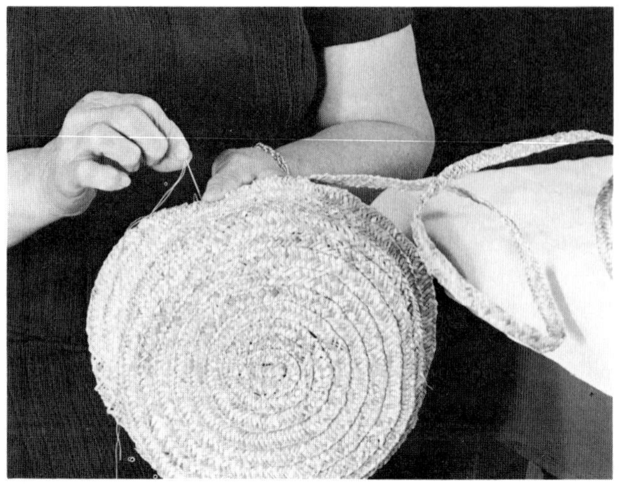

make your hat. It's a lot of work . . . it takes a full hour to make one yard of braiding and there's thirty yards of braid for a hat. And then there's two days to sew a hat together after it's braided. That much time is a lot to put into a hat!

But I get a lot of satisfaction out of it . . . I never sell any of them. I give them away . . . to friends and to my children. It's more rewarding to me to give something I've made to my children than if I went out and bought them something. It's the feeling of giving them something that you can't buy in the store . . . something made from your hands is more rewarding.

I have one granddaughter that's quite interested in this work. I'm hoping she'll learn. There is quite a few of the younger people that's trying to learn these old crafts which is very rewarding to me. If someone comes along and says, "I'd like to learn that," I want to show them because I'm not goin' to be around all these many years yet. If someone young learns it, probably the craft will stay . . . this is the way Mrs. Veinot felt when she learned me how to do it. An' that's the way I feel. I was a bit younger than she was, an' I'll keep it goin' a little while yet.

When the British founded Halifax in 1749, chip and straw hats were becoming very fashionable in England and Europe, and some of the settlers had come from straw hat-making centres. Those who settled in Halifax began supplying the fashion-conscious townspeople with fine imitations of Dunstable and Leghorn bonnets, while others who settled in the country made less imposing hats for their own use and sold any extra ones in nearby villages. Curiously, this handcraft has remained alive in the oral tradition in Nova Scotia, even though it has died out in many of the countries from which the settlers emigrated.

Straw hats, of "the cow's breakfast" variety, are braided of rye, oat or wheat straws. Rye is preferred because it is strong, thin and a good colour. Oat and wheat straws are often thicker and must be split before braiding. Only a few of the many different braiding patterns survive, one of which uses seven straws and is executed according to the ancient rhyme, "Over one and under two, Pull it tight and that will do."

Chip hats are braided with thin sheens of yellow birch. Jane Hiltz uses two different patterns for making her chip hats: a four sheen "four-strand-corner-edge braid" and a more complicated eight sheen "feather-edge braid."

Rush hats are braided in the same way as seven-strand straw hats, using long, pliable green rushes. These hats are relatively quick and easy to make, and many of the older residents of Lunenburg County can recall braiding rush hats when they were children.

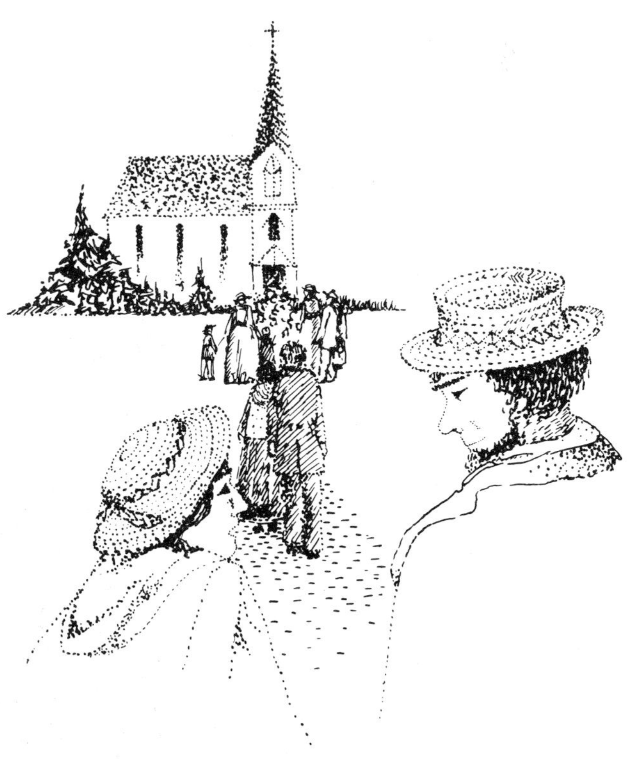

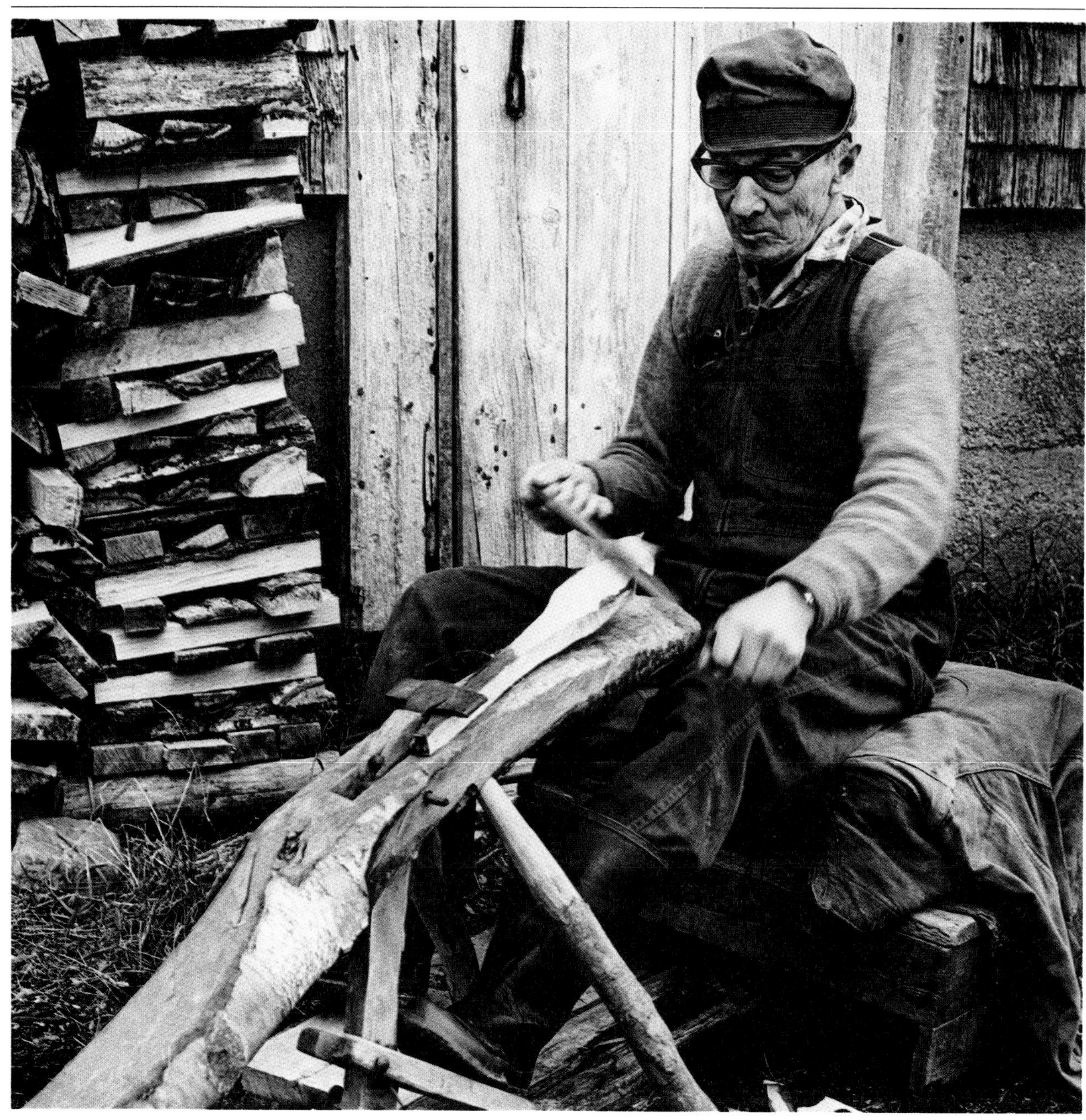

Alex Hiltz

Born 18 October 1907, Wooden Spoons

My old father, anything he could make out of wood – make himself – he never bought. Never paid a cent for anything that he could go out in the woods an' make. He'd go an' try to find the perfect piece o' wood or somethin' that was near enough to it. An' then he'd whittle it up. . . .

This one time – I was only young – I bought a wagon. An' I said to my father, "I'd like to have a long withe for my wagon. I wonder where a feller could get one?"

"Well," he says, "there's one right down there in the woods." An' I went down to the woods an' walked mostly all through it. I couldn't see no long withe – that's a reach pole for a wagon.

I came home an' I says, "I couldn't find one down there."

"I'll tell you what's wrong with you," the old man says, "you're lookin' for somethin' already made. And," he says, "you're not goin' to find it." I knew what he meant. I had no trouble findin' things – makin' things from there on in.

You kind o' visualize things in your head . . . how somethin' should be made. Now you take these spoons . . . Jane, my wife, always wanted me to make her a spoon. And I had a little slack time, and I had this in my mind anyway. So one day I started in. Thought I'd make a spoon . . . an' I didn't have no pattern or nothin'. I just visualized what a spoon should look like . . . an' that's the way I kept goin'. Never took a pattern off o' none – I just went ahead an' made a spoon. Had a mind of my own about what it was goin' to look like!

It's got to such a point that every-thin's got to be done in a big way. People have got so damn fussy and fancy. I can't see when you get right

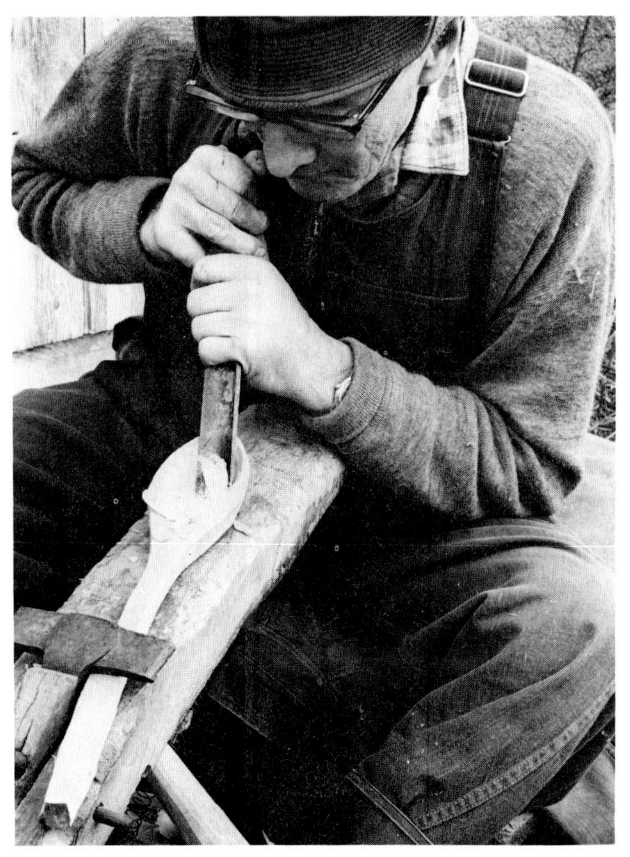

down to brass tacks where people's any better off than when they done things in the older ways. There's no job on earth that was done as good as the hands of a person can do.

Wooden spoon carving is a ubiquitous craft, and there is little historical documentation. There are several different styles of spoons made, depending on the tastes of the carver, or more likely, on those of his wife. Even with each carver, no two spoons are exactly alike, each one is made individually. The wood most often used is poplar, probably because of its softness, fine texture and light weight.

As Alex Hiltz explains, "The wood should generally be cut in the winter and set out some in the spring, but you should use it before it gets too dry an' tough. You split out a piece of wood, an' gouge it out to see if it's all right to make a spoon–you know pretty near what to take. Then you go an' hew it out a little with an axe. Lay it on the drawbench, an' use the drawknife some... change tools back an' forth as you go along... use the gouge awhile, then you see somethin' more you should do with the knife, an' you take up the drawknife an' use it for awhile. After it's dried out a little, it should be scraped or sanded–or both. That's about all there is to it."

Alex's wife, Jane, recommends seasoning the spoons in warmed cooking oil to keep the wood from splitting as it dries.

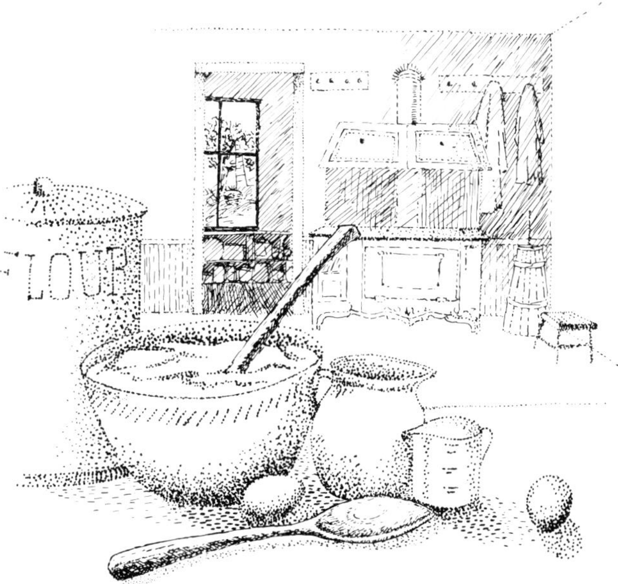

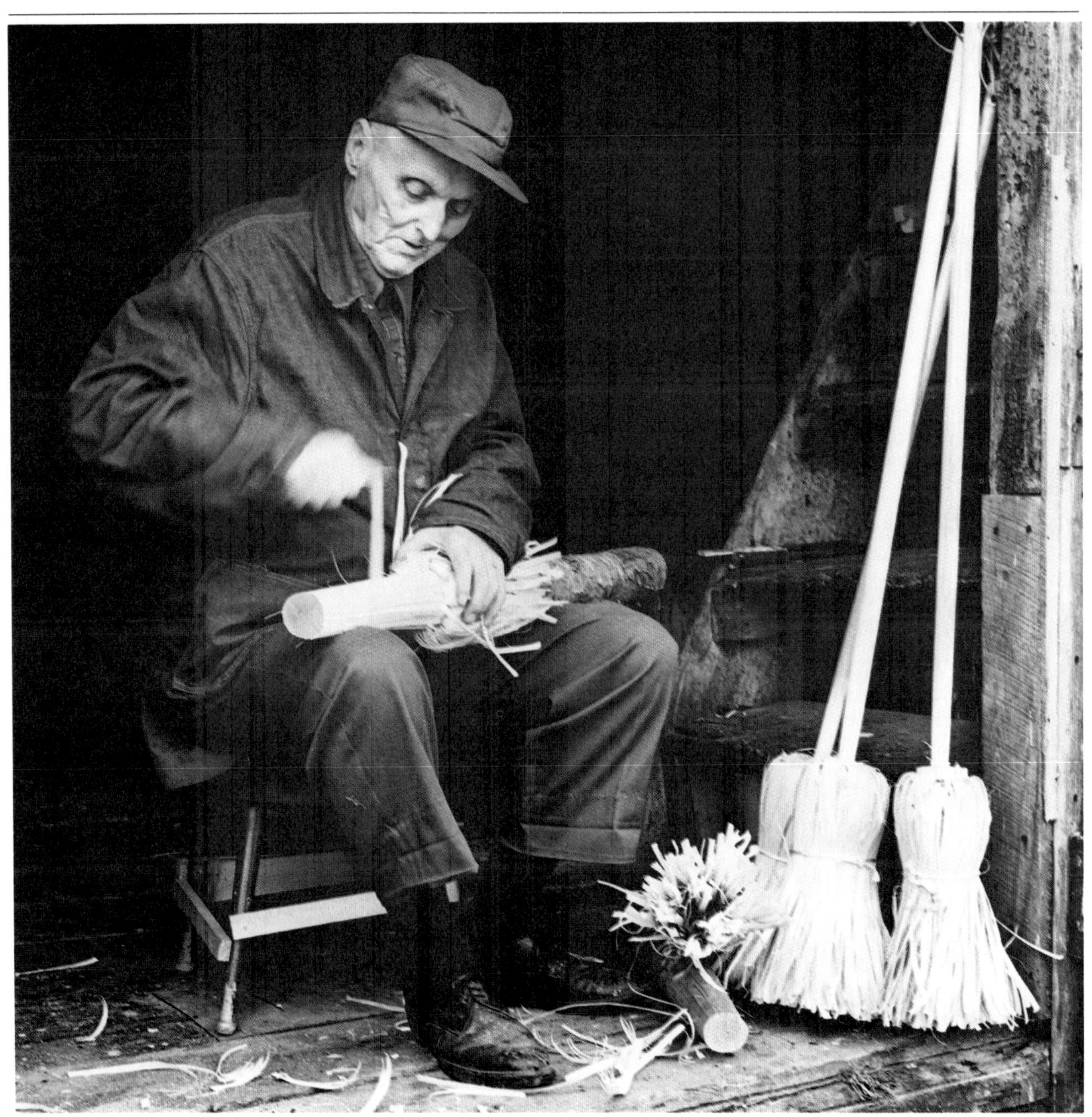

Clarence Keddy

Born 18 June 1894, Sheen Brooms

Now a lot of people have never seen a broom like this. There was one time a lot o' them around, but nobody makes 'em anymore. It's all one piece o' wood – start off with a good stick o' yellow birch an' that's all you need. See, you cut a collar here, maybe eleven inches from one end an' you take your sheens to that from the end, an' then you start sheening about fourteen inches the other way toward the collar an' that's what makes your broom head. Bend your sheens over, an' shave down your handle.

The Indians made 'em first. An' my uncle, I guess he learnt from them. He learnt me how to make 'em when I was eight or nine years old. Been makin' 'em for seventy, seventy-five years. Farmers used to use 'em to sweep out after the barn animals. An' then a while back, the women made 'em for to use on the vessels – that's all they used for brooms aboard the fishin' schooners. You had a hundred fifty sail o' vessels out o' Lunenburg, an' they always took about a dozen of them brooms to a vessel. Used 'em for washin' down the scuppers, the keds . . . the decks. An' for God sakes . . . them poor old women sheenin' all that birch, tryin' to make a few dollars. You'd see 'em with carts loaded wit' them brooms, takin' 'em into the firms to try to sell 'em. Sold 'em to Zwicker's an' Company, Knickles an' all them fellers. Ten cents apiece they used to get for 'em. Ten cents! An' it takes pretty near a day to make one. My God how things has changed!

I only make 'em for a pastime now. Somethin' to do. Some people still wants 'em – mostly for ornaments. I'm just doin' it passin' my time. Keeps me busy. But . . . see I like to work on all that stuff . . . you know, you can

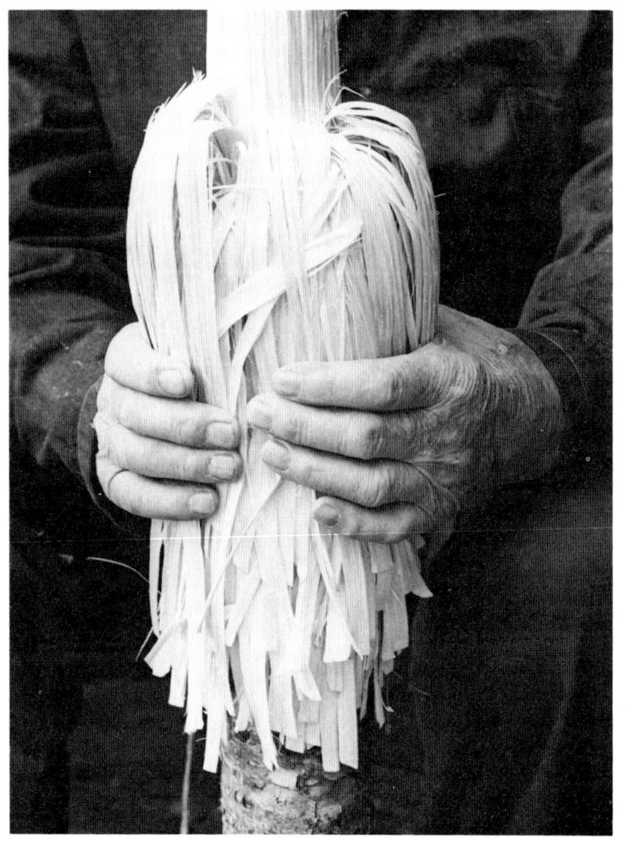

make a lot o' things yourself if you put your head to it. It's a nice feelin' workin' wit' wood.

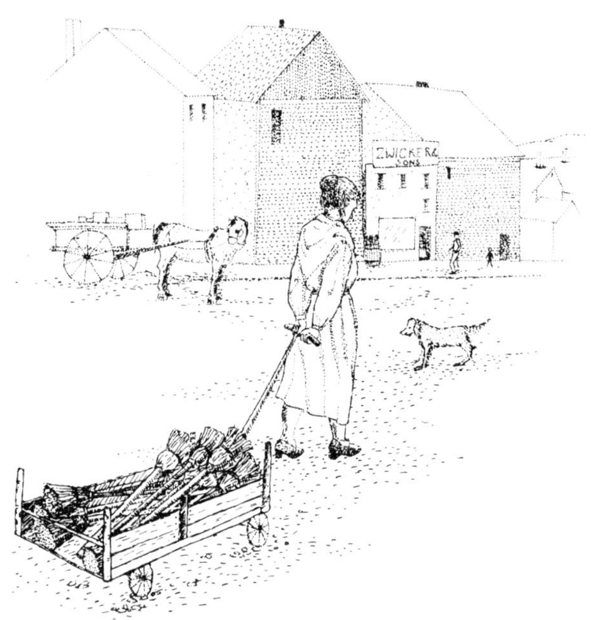

The origins of the sheen broom are lost in the dim mists of time. Some say that early Nova Scotian settlers learned the craft from the Micmac Indians. These brooms have also been found in the mountain communities of the southern United States. A. H. Eaton, in his *Handicrafts of the Southern Highlands* (1937), reported that men were making brooms of hickory and white oak by "... cutting the shavings from the handle, leaving them attached at one end and folding them back, bunched neatly." E. L. Horwitz, writing more recently (1974), observed men making what she referred to as "Appalachian hickory scrub brooms" in the same manner described by Eaton. Exactly when and from whom the craft was learned will probably never be known, but its execution seems to require the use of a sharp steel knife, suggesting it may have been a European introduction.

In Lunenburg County, they are known as "sheen brooms." In this area, the word "sheen" is used both as a verb and as a noun. As a verb, "to sheen" means to make a wooden strip by inserting a knife into the wood and pulling the chip down the length of the log. Used as a noun, "a sheen" refers to the strip of wood created by the process of sheening.

Clarence Keddy uses wirebirch or yellow birch to make his brooms, and his technique is more complex than that of the Appalachian broom-makers. Working with green wood, the bark is removed and the log is sheened at one end, pulling the strips toward the middle of the log. Rotating the log, the process is repeated again and again. The first few rounds of sheens are short, and they are discarded, but as the work progresses into the grain of the wood, the sheens become longer. When they are about eleven inches long, they are not drawn off, but left in place. Sheening continues, rotating the log until all that is left is a small centre core which is cut off. A collar is cut into the wood about half an inch deep just above the base of the sheens. Working from about the middle of the log, the wood is sheened towards the end of the log already worked. The sheens are pulled to within a few inches of the collar, bent over the previously made sheens, and held in place with a length of wire or rope. The ends of all the sheens are cut off evenly. To reduce the size of the log to a more manageable handle, the extra wood is carefully cut away with an axe and sanded smooth.

In this way, Clarence Keddy makes his brooms from one piece of wood. There are other broom-makers in Lunenburg County who make the handle and broomhead separately, assembling them later.

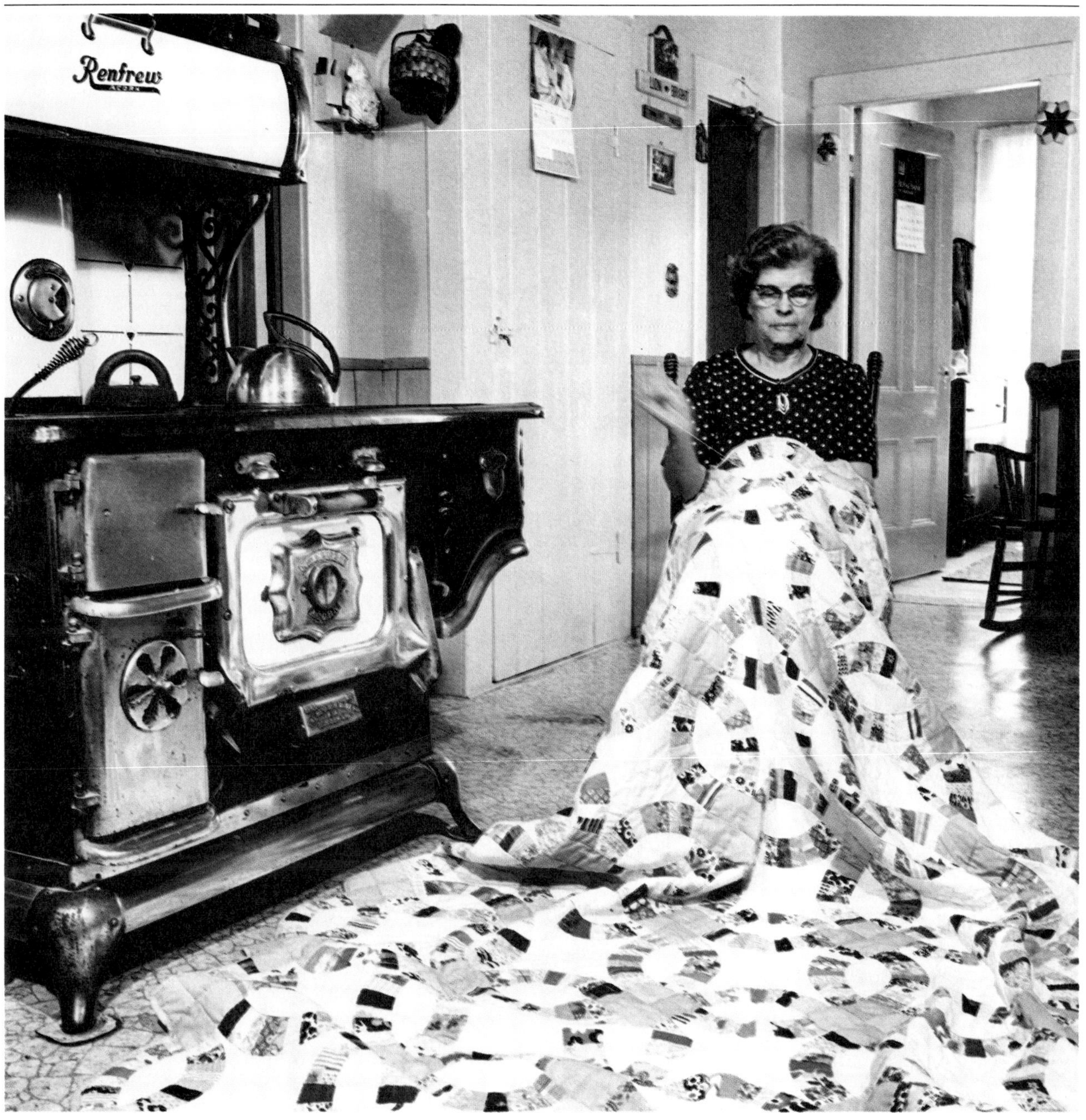
Renfrew

Grace Russell

Born 14 September 1906, Quilts

I used to . . . the first quilts I made was the crazy work ones. I guess it got its name "crazy work" 'cause you're crazy to do it! That's what we always used to call it – crazy work or patchwork. You don't have to have a pattern – just make it any way. Just use rags an' whatever old scraps you have layin' around from sewing. Saved up your scraps an' then in the winter . . . we'd all of us make quilts. Mum . . . she always made quilts. An' my sisters they could all make 'em.

I've spent a good many wintertime nights workin' on quilts. We used to have quiltin' parties too. Invite a lot o' women . . . have the quilt in the frames, an' quilt it. All quiltin' on the quilt. Then have a big supper – that's what they called a "quilting party." Oh, it was a lot o' fun. I enjoy makin' quilts . . . it's a pastime. I've always liked to make them. You always have somethin' to do after work.

Now, most of the quilts I get made I give away. I have eight children, an' I gave each one o' them one when they were married . . . then I gave each of them one for Christmas presents. But not all at one time! Then with the first-born in each family . . . in the families when their babies came, one quilt . . . a baby quilt. I give each family one regardless of how many children they have. I give them one quilt for the first child. Then you see, that quilt gets handed down . . . it would last right through for all o' them. Giving them to my children and my grandchildren . . . that's my pleasure. I enjoy that.

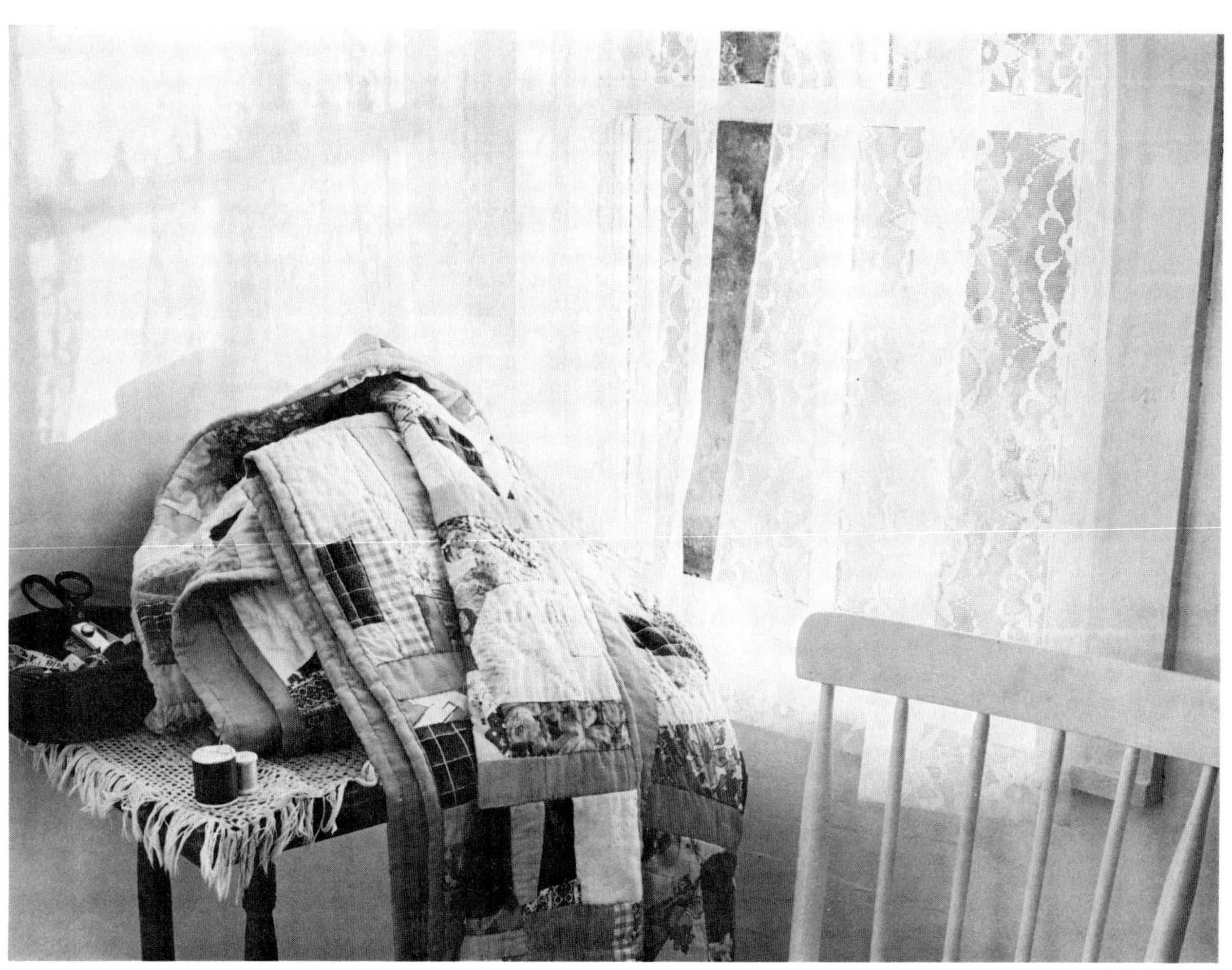

Quilting was one of the needle arts brought to Nova Scotia by early European settlers. They were familiar with patchwork and appliqué designs and with quilted wall hangings, bedcovers and undergarments. For the settlers, the quilted bedcover or "quilt" was a utilitarian object, very plainly constructed of heavy material, which would last the wear of several generations.

Making a quilt involves stitching three layers of fabric together–backing, liner and top. In the early days of Nova Scotia, the backing was usually one piece or several pieces of cloth sewn together. The liner was ordinarily a hand-carded wool fleece batt. The top was a very simple four- or nine-patch design, using squares of homespun material cut from worn or castoff clothing. When the top layer wore thin, it was recovered with another patterned top. In some cases, this would happen several times to one quilt, so that it became a record of the kinds of material and styles of clothing that the family had worn over a span of several years. Today, the backing and top are frequently colour coordinated materials purchased especially for the purpose. The batts may be cotton, but polyester is more common.

There are few, if any, patterns unique to Nova Scotia, because quilt blocks were brought here from the United States and England. A favourite pattern down through the years has been the "crazy quilt", made with odd scraps of cloth in no set pattern arrangement. Other popular patterns include those based on the square and the triangle, and on the variations of light and dark, plain or patterned pieces. One such pattern is the "Double Wedding Ring", which Grace Russell is working on in the photograph.

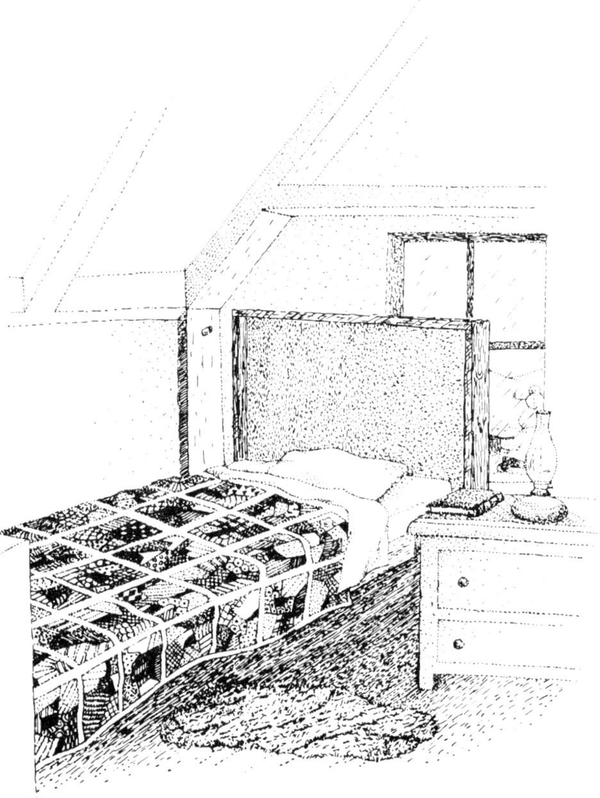

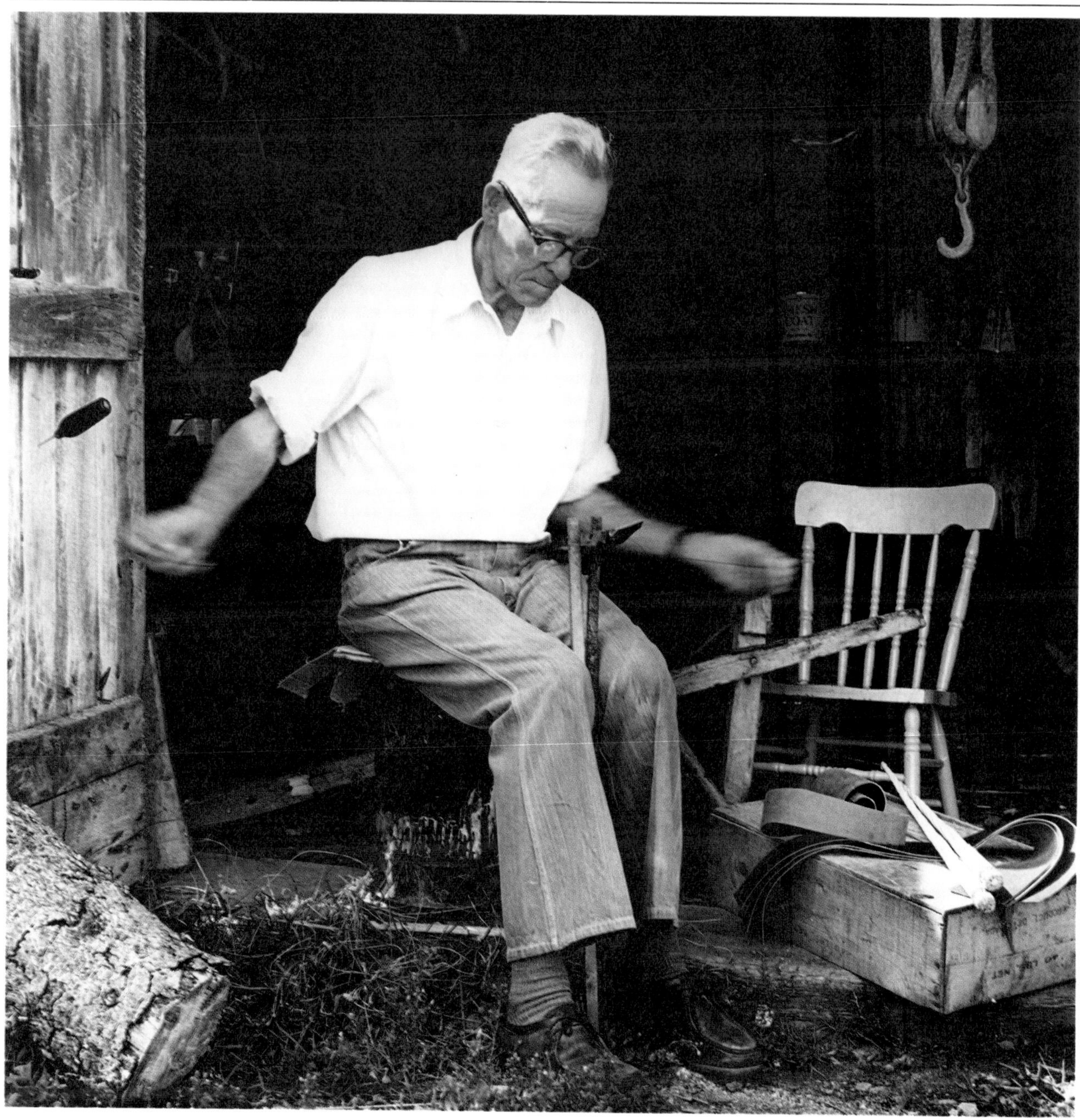

Stanley Russell

Born 8 August 1905, Ox Whips

I always made my own whips. Now some fellers maybe, they couldn't make one the way it should be. But most generally, there was always somebody around the settlement that would make 'em. Everybody had whips 'cause most everybody had teams of oxen. If we went back to them days, it would be quite a turnover, I imagine.

Years ago, every farm here had a yoke of oxen and some had two. Back twenty-five, thirty years ago, we all had oxen 'cause they done the heavy work for us. There was no tractors in them days. Oxen done all the work on the farm, ploughin', harrowin', makin' hay. . . . An' . . . I often think back . . . there'd be as high as ten or twelve loads of apple barrels goin' to the Valley an' all with oxen. They'd haul 'em clean from this side o' Chester – take three or four days for a trip. Camp along the road. An' we used to log the oxen down to Aldersville. There'd be fifteen or twenty teams in a string in the wintertime goin' through the woods. We'd all set out across the lakes. When we was out on the lake . . . line up, look at the teams loaded with logs on. See who had the best logs on an' who had the biggest loads on. They'd have anywhere from seven hundred to a thousand feet – that was solid lumber. Haulin' lumber to the mills. Then you'd go into the woods an' cut your year's firewood before the snow came, then haul it out with the teams on the snow on sleds an' pile it in the barns.

Today it's all tractors . . . faster, easier. With a team . . . it takes a lot o' skill to run 'em. Some teams you can just speak to 'em . . . the less whip you use on 'em – within reason – the better. They have to know you mean 'em to get to work – to mind you.

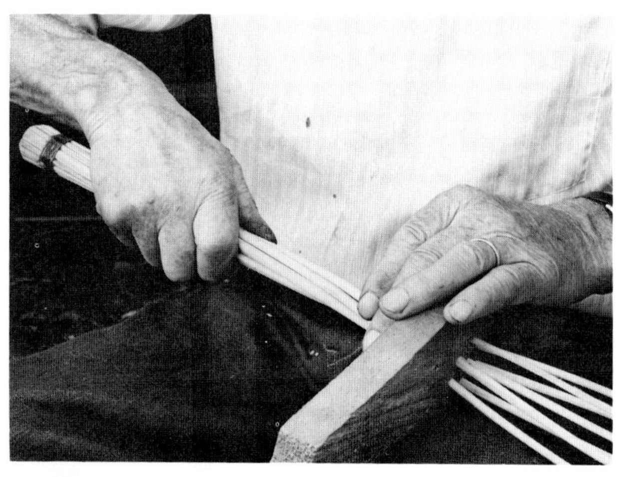

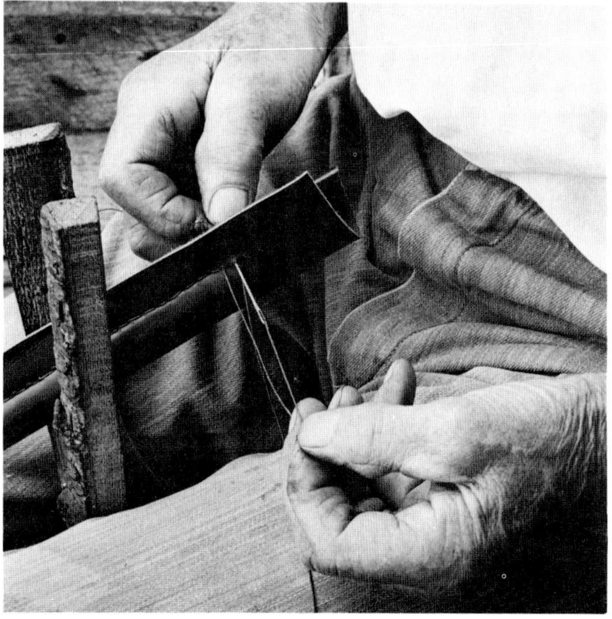

There's not two teams alike. They're always just a little different. You get to know the ways of 'em an' they get to know the teamster. Oh, you can do the work quicker with a tractor. . . 'course it does cost you more.

Anyways, the younger generation is goin' off the farms for the factories . . . places like that. The farms are all goin' to pieces. An' that's the way it will all end. The whips I make now. . . well, it's kind of a hobby. . . more than anything, it helps to pass the time.

The making of ox whips was carried on by one or two men in the community to supply their own needs and those of their fellow teamsters. The whip-makers in Nova Scotia today use at least three different techniques in making the handle-foundation. The first involves splitting a piece of wood into twelve strands, which are then braided. In the second, the wood is split into a smaller number of strands to almost the full length of the stick, leaving the last six or eight inches uncut, and then twisting them. The third technique involves splitting the wood completely into separate strands and then twisting them tightly together.

Stanley Russell uses the third method. A long piece of ash, about one and a half inches across and three feet long, is cut and then quartered the full length of the stick. The quarters are split and shaved down into seven strands, with one strand being larger than the others. The strands are arranged with the larger strand in the centre and the others around it, and they are tied with strong twine at the butt ends. After pouring hot water over the wood to soften it, the strands are inserted as far as they will go into a piece of wood with six, equally spaced holes cut in a circle, with a seventh hole in the centre. Holding the end of the handle firm, the strands are rotated as they are pulled through the wood, twisting them until they are tight. The tips of the strands are tied firmly to prevent them from untwisting.

The handle is covered with leather: "You don't want too heavy a leather, but a good tough leather, somethin' that won't stretch too much." After cutting a tapered length to cover the handle, the seam is sewn using a single piece of strong thread.

The leather of the whip is different from that used in the handle. It is what Stanley refers to as "Indian-tanned," a very pliable leather which he purchases in half-inch wide strips. He cuts small slits along the mid-line of a strip and folds it back on itself through the slits to make what he calls "belt-lacin'." A short length of quarter-inch leather and a slightly longer piece of heavy twine are attached to the end of the whip to complete the work.

The whips are not used heavily by most teamsters, many of them prefer to talk to their oxen and use the whips as gentle reminders of their commands.

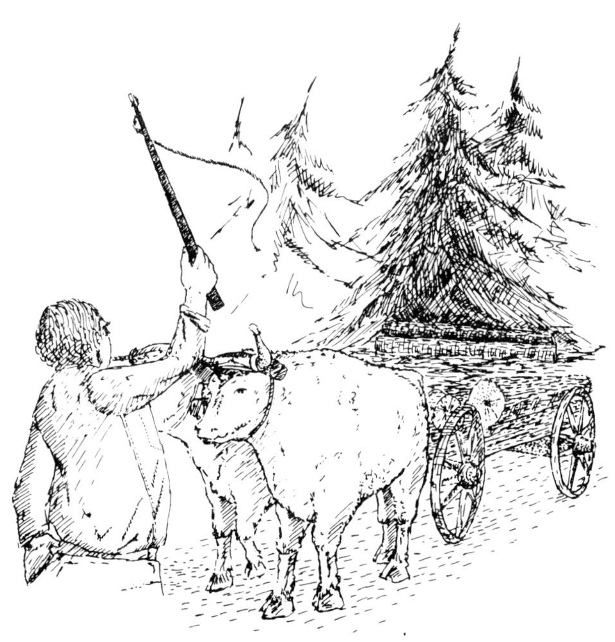

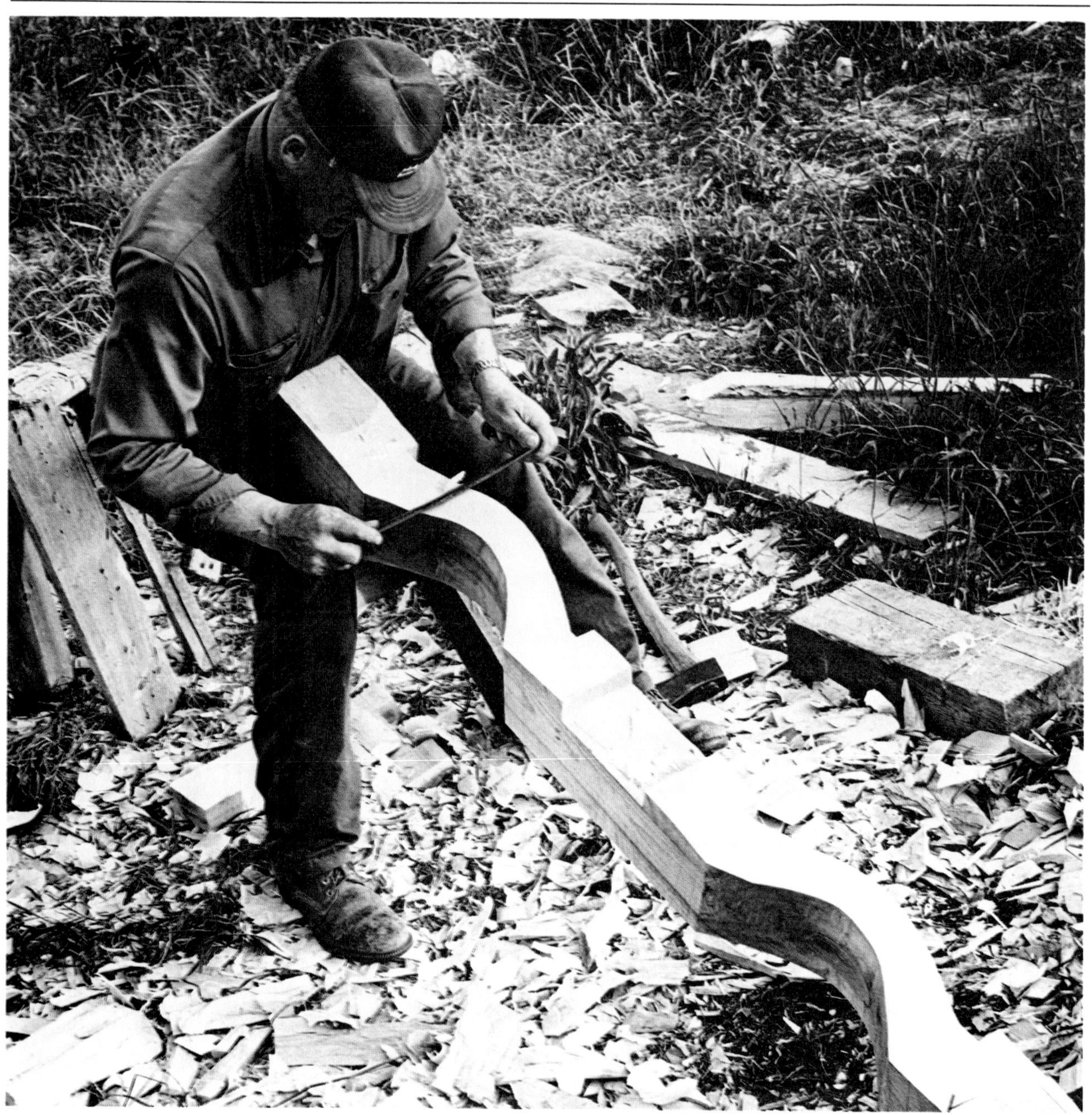

Grover Boland

Born 20 November 1922, Ox Yokes

Years ago around here, used to be three – 'round three hundred ox teams in the woods in wintertime. You know, workin' haulin' pulp wood an' logs. An' then in the summer, we used to go for meadow hay – we'd go in the mornin' early, take our dinner an' our hand scythes an' our oxen, wagon an' go. An' we'd come home at night – we done that for days an' days, long as the weather was fine. Have kayaks for dinner an' when you got home you'd have beans an' potatoes for supper. You know, hodge podge they call it. I believe to gosh we lived better then, to tell the truth . . . you know . . . we didn't have as much but what we had, we had.

Anyways, Farish Frederics – he's dead now but, oh God, he'd be in his nineties – he used to come to our barn. This was in the thirties – an' he'd make three yokes in one day. Bring his horse an' wagon, an' we'd have the wood – you had to have the wood yourself. An' he'd start off an' he'd make three a day 'fore he was finished. That's a lot o' chippin', I'm tellin' you. Start off with a piece o' wood about six feet long an' square it, y'know, square it an' you measure the heads o' the oxen so you know what size you want in the heads an' beam. There's no way you could do anything with machinery – all we use is a drawknife an' an axe, chisel, handsaw, an' a gouge. Old Farish'd come in our barn an' make three a day. He'd make three yokes in one day an' fit 'em on – each pair of oxen is different an' the yoke has to fit just right. Yes, that's a lot o' chippin'. Was from daylight to dark too. Just stopped for him to eat. That was his trade, you know what I mean, at that time. You had to call him an' he'd tell us what day he'd come – an' you had your work ready an' he'd hit there an' the

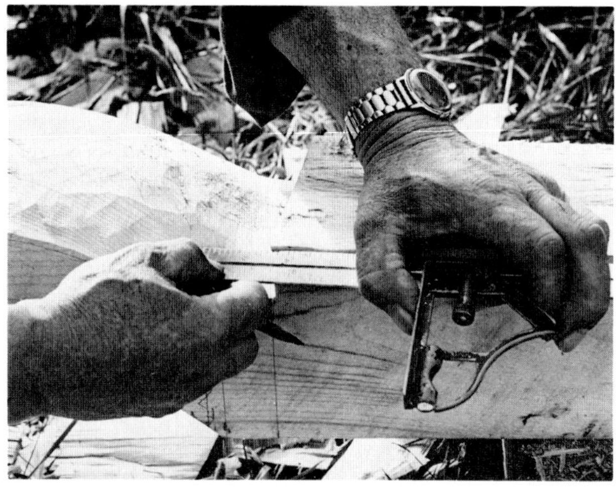

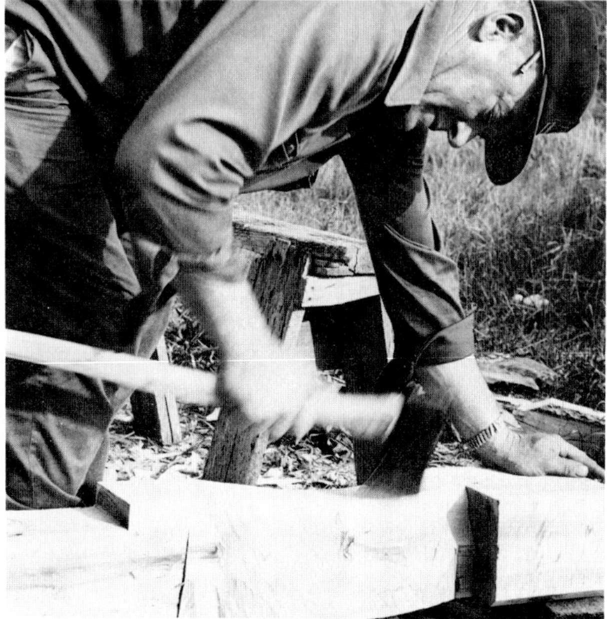

next day go on to another feller.

Well, when he'd come, I'd watch him – oh, I guess I was about twelve years old. I'd whittle just small ones out of a piece o' wood with my jackknife. That's how I learned, watchin' him make 'em. I enjoy makin' 'em 'cause I . . . the more I do it, the better I'm gettin' at it. I like to make 'em. Years ago, everybody made a different one, you know, a different shape. There's not too many alike y'know. It's just for . . . for a feller's own pride, you know . . . to make 'em different ways.

But now there's not enough oxen around to make a livin' at it. I tried to get my son at it, but . . . I don't think he even ever tried to make one. He set an' watched me a little. Maybe some day he might . . . you know . . . try it. It's too bad some young feller wouldn't take it up, you know . . . part time, mind you, for the oxen that is still around.

The use of oxen has had a long history in Nova Scotia. Their even temperament, sure-footedness, strength and generally docile manner made them the preferred animal for hauling timber, ploughing fields and pulling heavy wagons to market. Over the years, they were gradually replaced by horses, but the lure of keeping a team is strong even today. There are several teams in the province reserved for occasional use on the land but more so for the excitement of ox-pulls at summertime exhibitions.

Oxen can be worked singly or in pairs. The teamsters, according to Grover Boland, would "...usually try to get the oxen the same size an' try to get 'em marked as close the same as possible–colour, you know. That goes way back to the old times. Everybody tried to get a pair alike–they'd even trade. They all took great pride in tryin' to get the best."

The oxen would be trained to work as a team from a very young age. The first yoke was usually made of poplar because of its light weight, but as the animals grew in size and strength, the yokes would be made of a hardwood such as yellow birch. Each year, the oxen needed a new yoke, for they quickly outgrew its close fit.

There were a number of different styles of yokes used in the province, but the one made by Grover Boland is called a "Dutch yoke." A yellow birch log, about six feet long, is squared off and the distances between the oxen, the size of their heads and horns are carefully measured and marked off on the wood, which is then cut away with an axe, saw, drawknife, chisel and gouge. Because both oxen in a pair are not of equal size, the yoke-maker must determine the centre of balance: "If one ox is bigger, they usually make the yoke longer on that side, an' give the little one the shorter end of the yoke."

The fit of the yoke is very important: "You gotta have it so it fits good, so it doesn't pinch 'em, an' it isn't too tight. If it don't fit right, they can't work it... some o' them'll haul it off, split it apart, if the horns ain't tipped just right. An' then, if it's the other way, they crowd together... you gotta get 'em to fit just right."

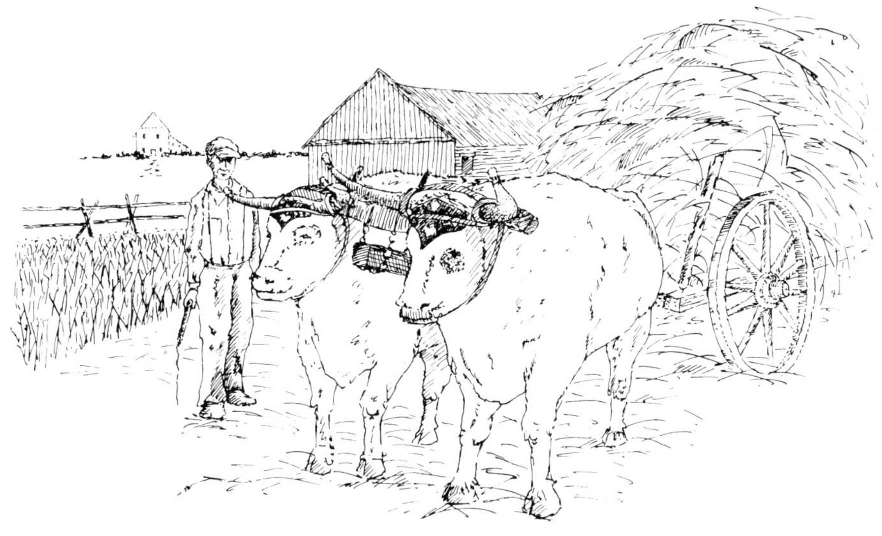

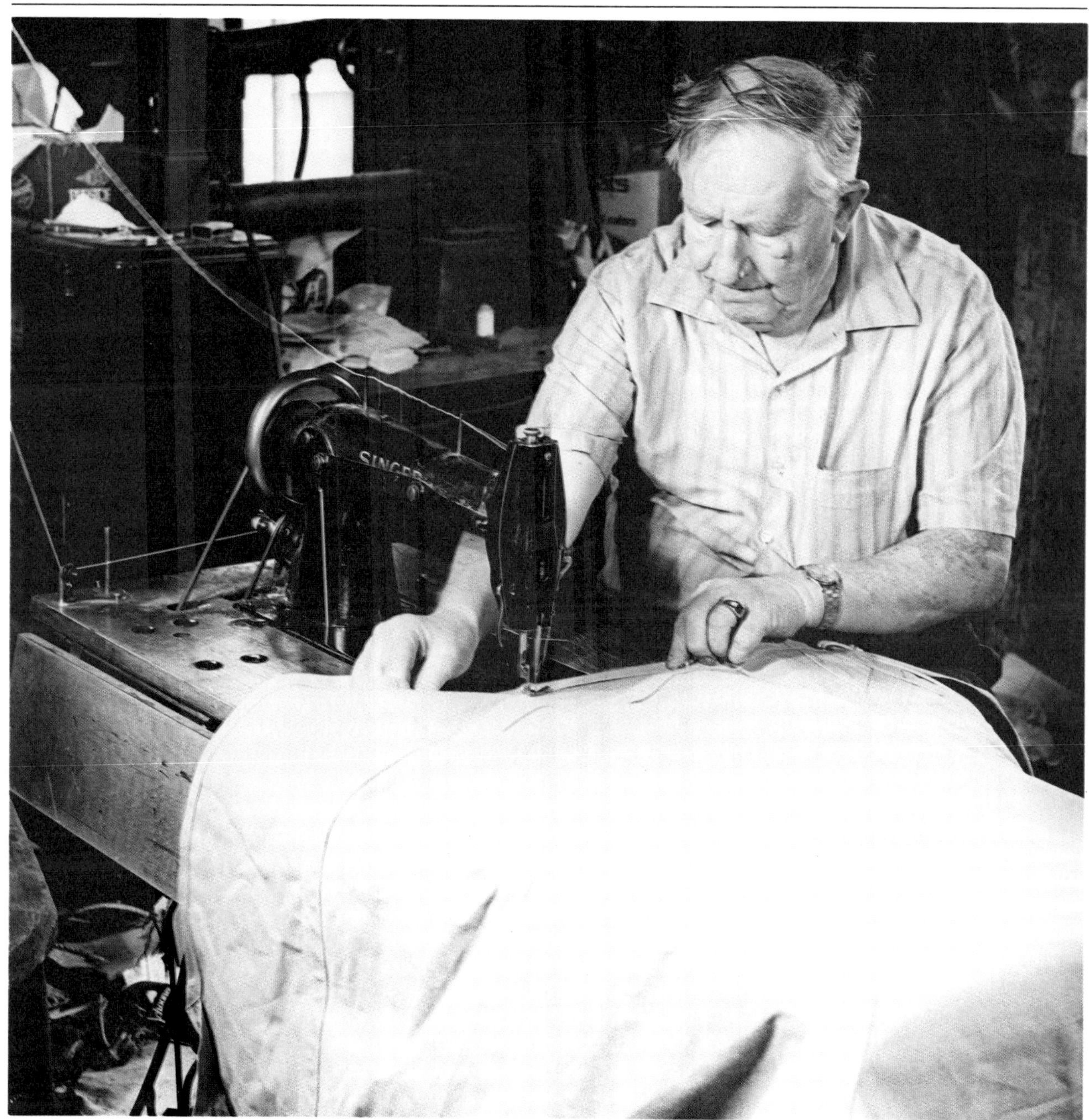

Everett Lohnes

Born 12 June 1901, Sail-Maker

I been sixty-three years bein' a sail-maker. Fourteen years old when I started in – you got a dollar an' a half a week. Ten hours a day. Fourteen years I was. That's sixty-three years. That's right.

At that time there was nothin' else but fishermen – fishermen an' fishin' schooners. Why in the 1930s, we had around a hundred and thirty vessels out o' Lunenburg, an' all the sail work was done here an' the other place – Hebb over in the sail loft in the lower strait. Two sail lofts in town at that time, an' both of 'em employed eight or nine men. These two sail lofts, they made all the sails for the vessels in Lunenburg an' around everyplace. They'd have a suit of sails made for on a new vessel, an' when it'd come home from fishin' in the fall of the year . . . if there was anythin' to be done to that suit of sails, they'd bring 'em to the sail loft here and store 'em for the winter for repairs. A vessel'd keep a suit of sails about three years, an' then they would come back for a new suit.

I've seen 'em come an' go. From the big fleet to nothin'. Why, I helped to make sails for *Bluenose I*. Mains'l had forty-one cloths into it. Forty-one cloths twenty-two inches wide. That'd be seventeen or eighteen hundred yards of stitchin'. Three or four weeks for a full suit of sails – all handmade. Eight men workin' on 'em. Had a couple o' men that could stitch twenty-five yards an hour. That's a lot o' stitchin'. Now there's nothin'. Oh, I make sails for the shore fishin' boats, little jiggers for the aft end of the boat. Riding sails. Nothin' like it was. I'm here alone now . . . an' the vessels is gone.

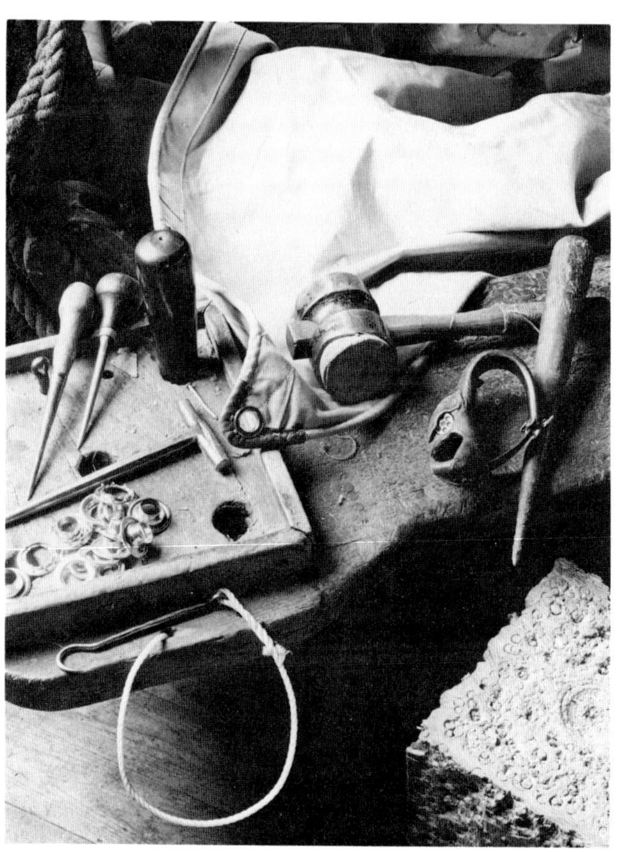

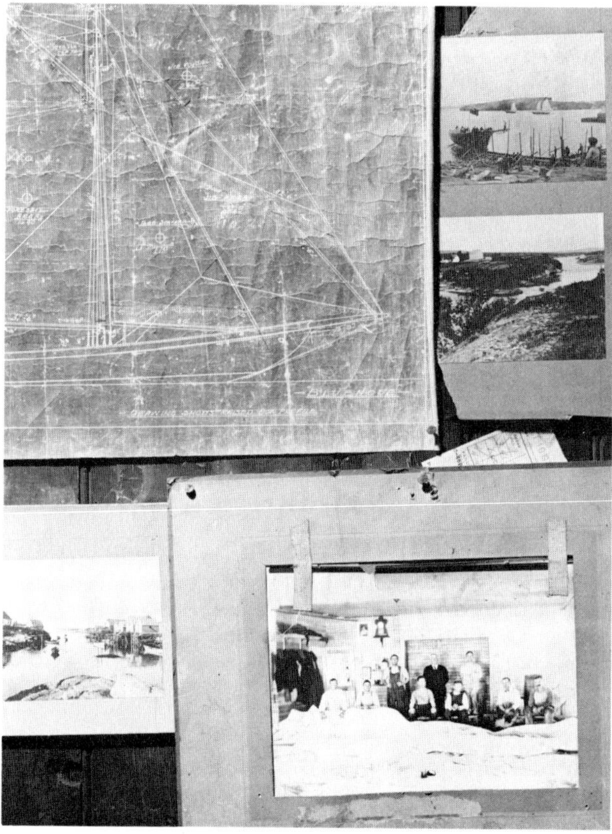

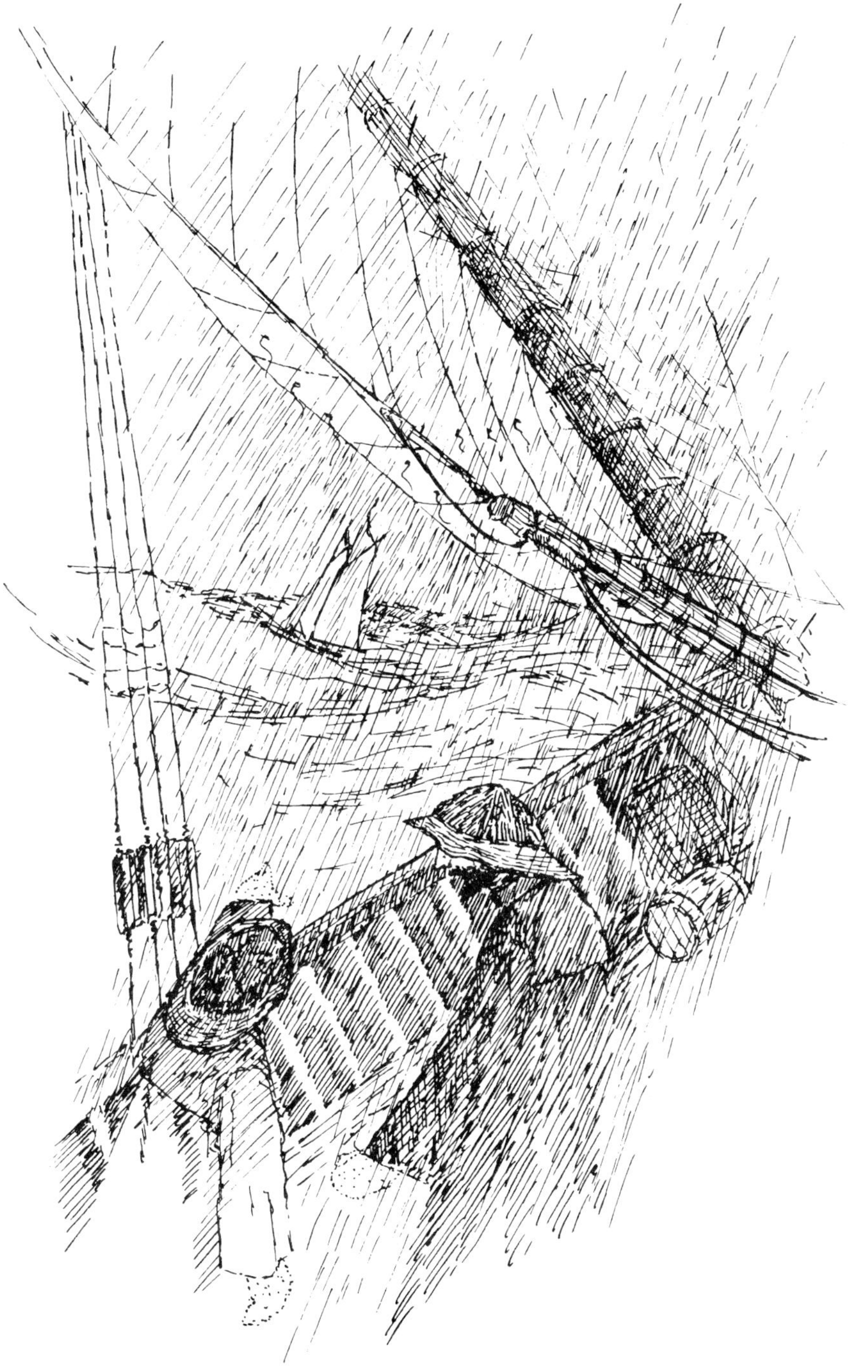

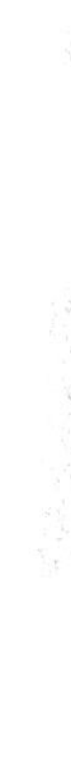

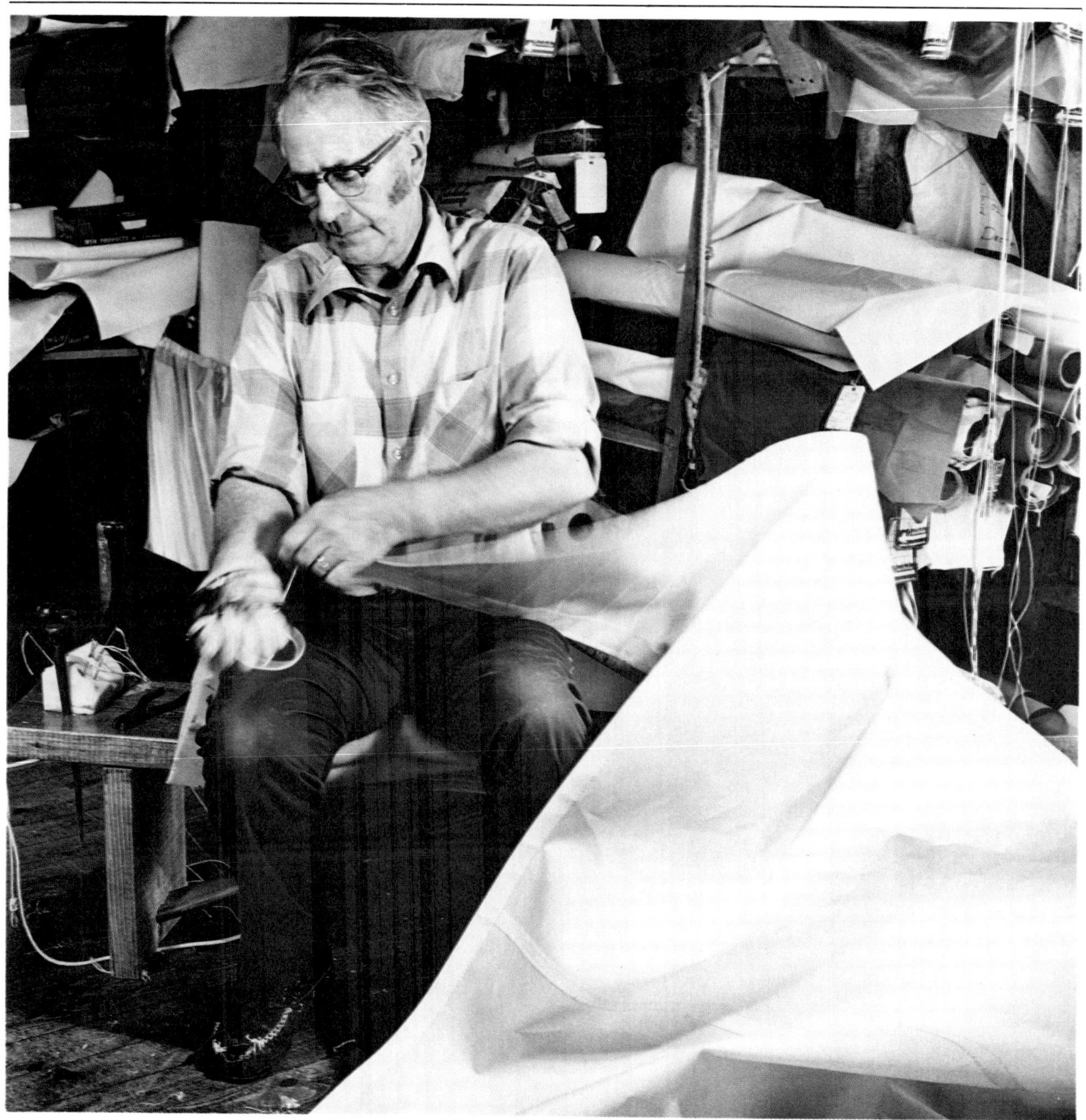

Harold Stevens

Born 13 July 1911, Sail-Maker

My father started out on Tancook Island. He thought, "Here's my father buildin' boats, why can't I make sails?" So he started up on his own, no help. Makin' sails for the forty-, fifty-, sometimes sixty-foot deck boats. Deck boats, that's what they used to call them. An' there was a lake out there on the island an' he'd lay those big sails out on the ice, an' sewed 'em up by hand an' roped 'em. You see, there was no buildings out there big enough to lay 'em out in so he'd use the ice. Didn't mind the cold a bit. Now, you can make sails from a plan – draw up a plan an' cut each piece out individually, but it's simpler if you can just mark your corners – say drive a nail in the ice for each corner of the sail an' put a string around to mark off the sail an' cut it that way. It's much simpler. My dad was no man to do things complicated if there was a simpler method to do it. An' that was the simpler method.

Anyway, we moved in here to the mainland an' bought this farm. An' I guess I was in grade eight an' dad took me out o' school about midway through the season an' said, "You got to come home an' help me make sails." Well, I left school to make sails. We had a large family – twelve children – an' dad needed everybody that could help to help. I didn't mind at all. I liked it. I liked makin' sails. I helped him then – I stood behind the sewin' machine an' pulled the cloth as he sewed it. You see, a big heavy sail, it bundles up, bundles up on you. So I just kept movin' the cloth as the sewin' machine sewed it. That was my job, my part of it.

Well, about that time – in the 1920s – we were switchin' from fishing sails to yacht sails. Fishin' vessels – sailin' vessels – were on their way out. And that's what I'm makin'

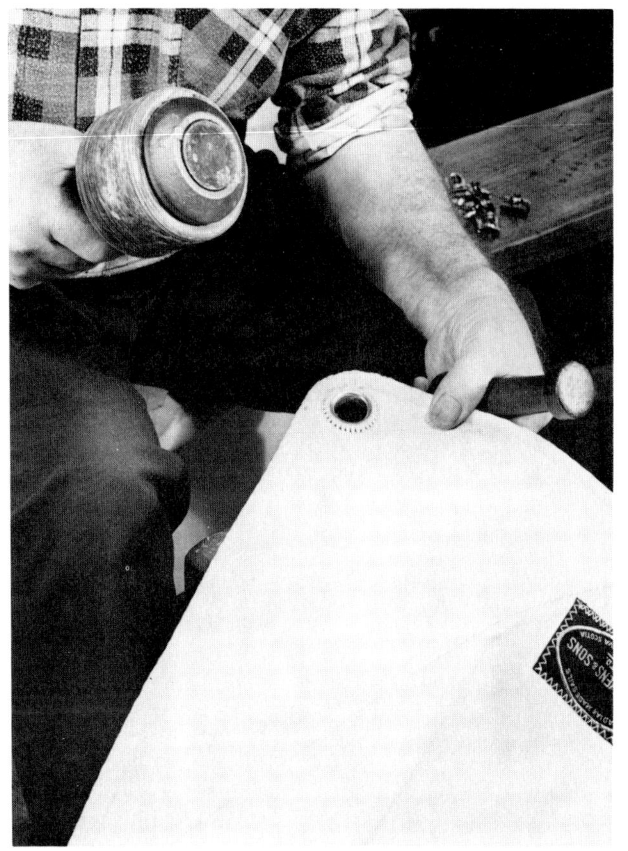

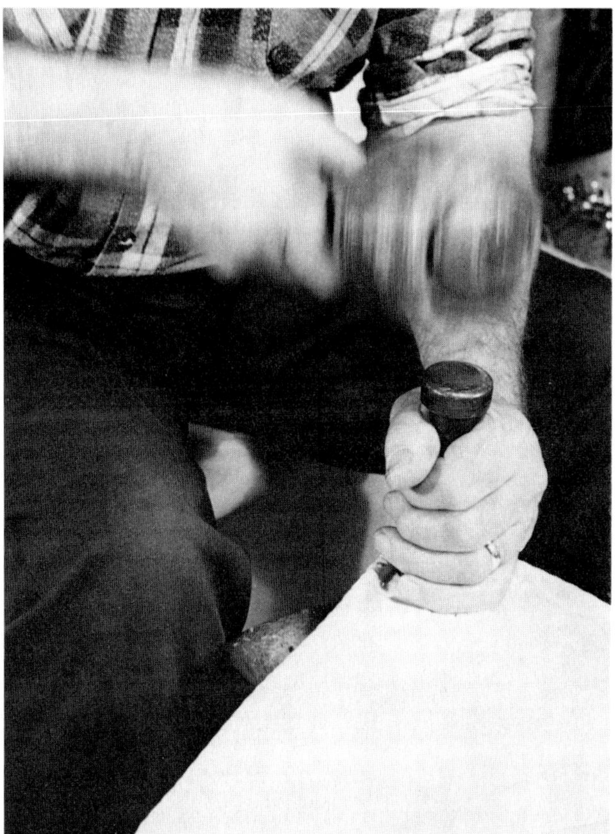

now – sails for yachts. It's a challenge for me. In days gone by in the fishing industry, anything went. It was a sail an' they hoisted it – as long as it made the boat go, that was it. But with a yacht sail, there's more skill and calculation involved. If you make a sail – somethin' good, that's at a par with a great sail-maker, or a great sail-making company – it's rewarding.

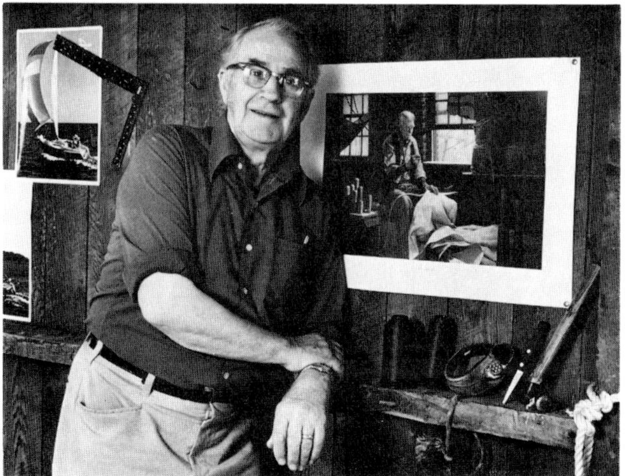

Although we know that the Royal Navy sailed with flax sails in the mid-eighteenth century, there is little recorded evidence of the kind of sails used by the first fishing settlers in Nova Scotia. Their sails were most likely made of linen cloth imported from England. It was not until the late eighteenth century that the cotton industry in the southern United States was established, and cotton canvas became cheaper than English linen canvas. The term "canvas" refers to the tightness of the weave, not to the fibre used in the cloth.

Everett Lohnes makes cotton canvas sails in the old way. His sails are used by inshore fishermen on the stern of their motor boats, "... to keep 'em head to the wind." The canvas is sold in bolts of varying widths, none of which is the size of the finished sail, so the sail is made up by piecing together several lengths of cloth. The size of the finished sail is marked off on a large floor with a nail in each corner. A string is drawn around each of the three markers and the canvas is unrolled. Everett makes his seams parallel to the leach of the sail: "You cut from the smallest cloth until you get to the biggest one, you keep on goin'...," unrolling the bolt again and again parallel to the first cut, always allowing extra cloth for seam allowances, until the triangular area is filled. The lengths are then carefully sewn together on his straight-stitch sewing machine. The edges are trimmed, stitched and roped. The sails are tanned to prolong the life of the cotton canvas.

In contrast, Harold Stevens represents a family that began sail-making in 1908, and as he says, "We put ourselves in the phasing out of one type an' following right into the other... from sail-making with canvas, to the Egyptian cotton and on to the dacron. In the days when my father was young, anythin' went. Their sails had streaks into 'em, flat spots, tight spots or full spots into 'em... it didn't make any difference... it was a sail an' they hoisted it, an' that was it... as long as it made the boat go. They had a mains'l, a jib an' a fors'l. There was no such thing as loose-footed sails, it was all booms, an' it was almost self-tending. They didn't go into the engineerin' of a sail... it was there an' they sailed by it. There was no foolin' around or experimentin' with sails, you know, to get two minutes faster than the next guy. Now, with racin' sails, it's a challenge... anythin' you can do to a sail to get ahead of another one, that's really competitive and it's fun."

Racing sails are made in basically the same way as the old sails; they are composed of panels of cloth sewn together, but the arrangement of the panels is more complex, the materials are different, and the measurements and calculations have to be more exact. Synthetic fibres are used now, and the computer has recently been introduced for more precise measurement. Zigzag sewing machines sew the panels together and the edges are generally taped, although some are roped. The benchman uses aluminum headers and metal grommets along the edges of the sail, where they will slide into metal tracks in the boom and mast. Racing sails are advanced pieces of technology, and Harold Stevens is well respected for his sail-making abilities that are based on his many years as a traditional sailmaker.

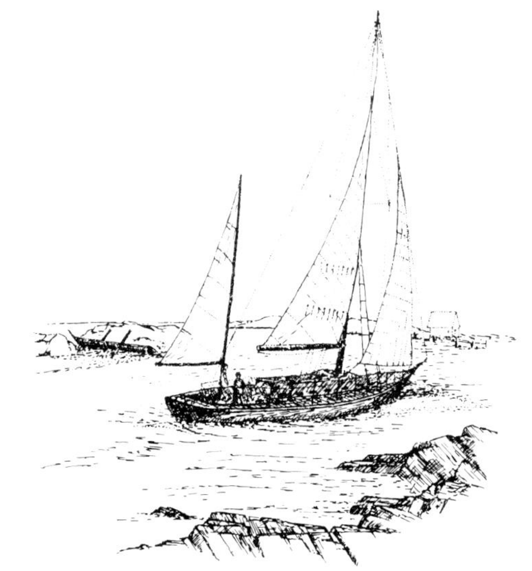

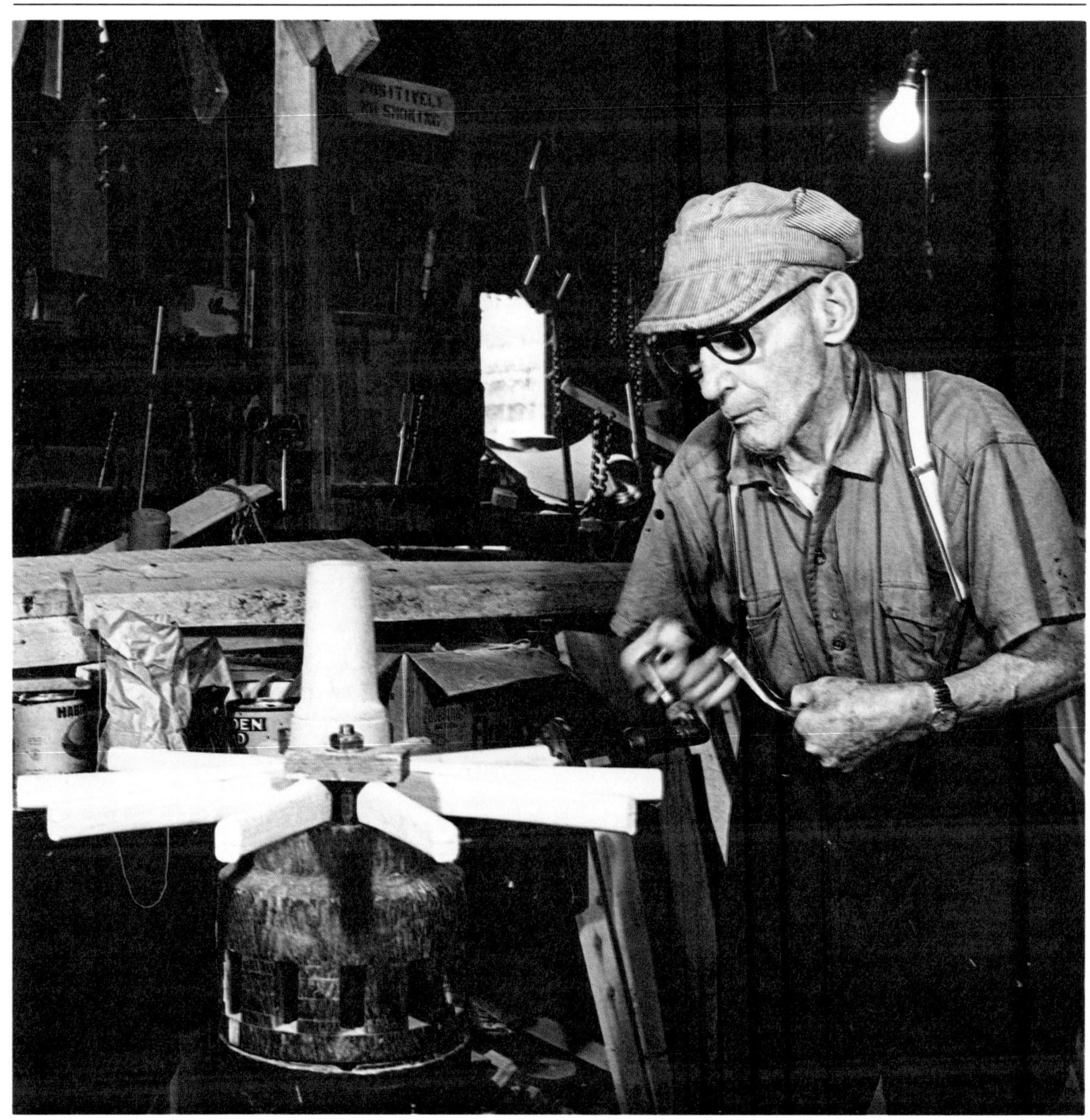

Arthur Ernst

Born 18 May 1894, Wheelwright

I started off wit' my father makin' wagons for oxen an' horses – we made dozens an' dozens of 'em. In them days there was no cars an' all the travel an' the work on the farms was done . . . everybody had a horse or a team of oxen. An' then in the summertime we went out to build sawmills in the woods . . . had to put the posts down an' sills an' floors an' the roof – the whole works – an' then we put in the machinery. Yes sir, start right from scratch an' build the whole darn thing. Why we even built the wheels that run the machinery. An' repairin' – I seen a lot o' repairin' on the mills that was around. An' there was a lot of 'em, that I can tell you. A lot of lumberin' an' a lot of mills to saw the lumber.

All them mills is gone now. I can still make most anythin' that comes along. Anythin' that can be made of wood I can make, an' I don't think there's many men that can stand next to me in that way. No sir! An' as far as I know, for miles an' miles around, I'm the last wheelwright. 'Course the wheels I make now ain't nothin' like them big wheels in the mills. Just playthings – wheels for wheelbarrows an' like that.

After I'm gone, there's nobody around to take up this business at all. I done it all my life – but I'm goin' on eighty-three now an' sometimes I get a little tired. I'm tryin' to work twelve hours a day an' it tuckers me out some. An' you know, it's funny when I'm sleepin', I dream about my work. Dream about the things that puzzle me. Funny, ain't it?

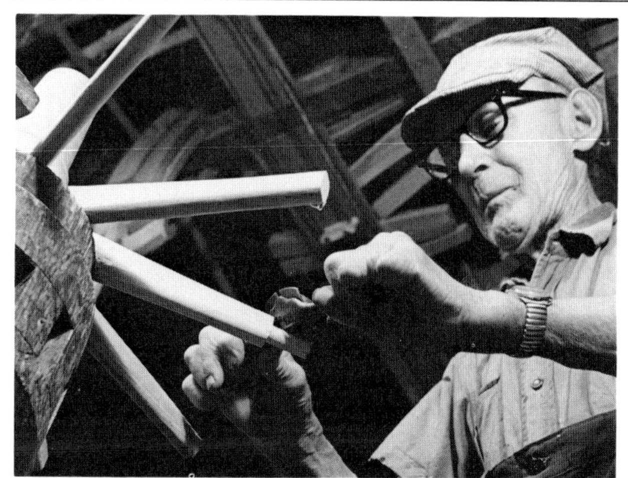

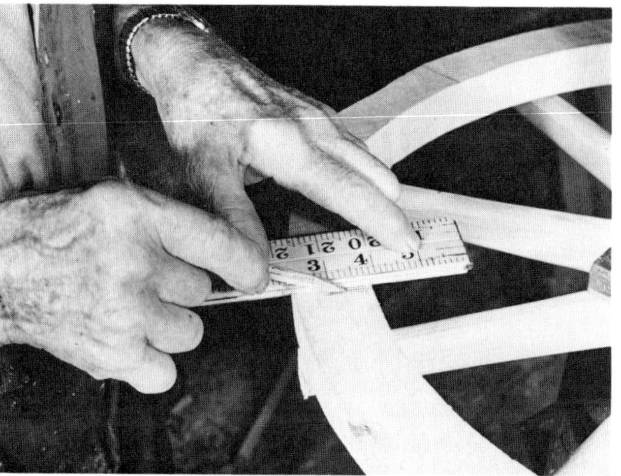

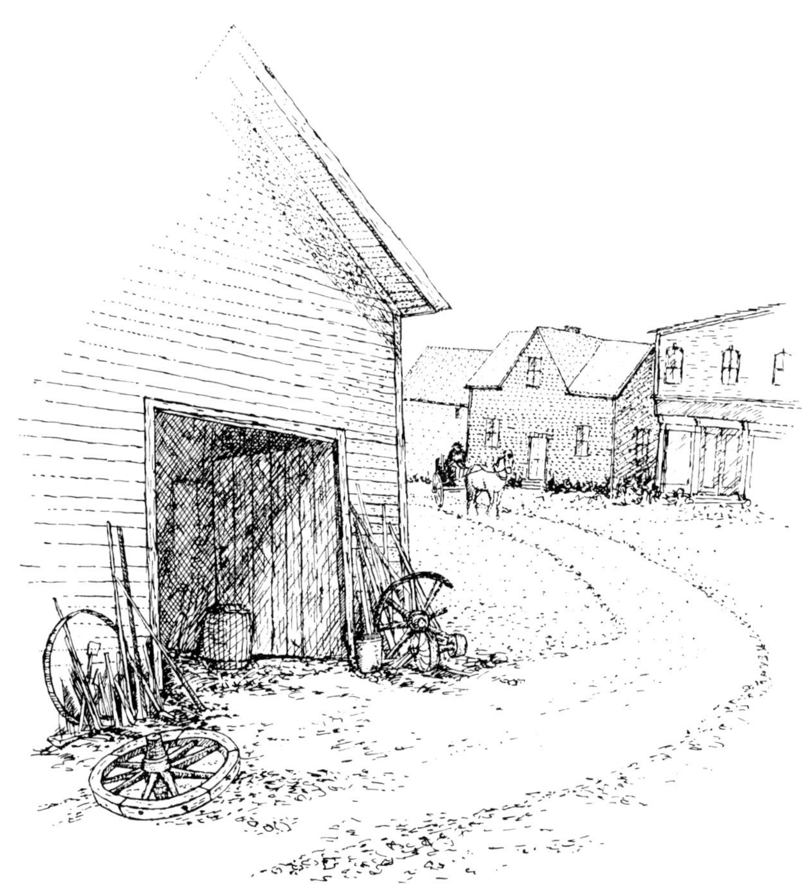

Arthur Ernst is matter-of-fact about making his wheels, which is not really surprising when you consider that he has been making all kinds for most of his eighty-three years: "Well, you take a piece of wood an' cut it in the lathe, an' you turn the hub...." It all sounds so simple, yet his choice of wood, its seasoning, the angle of his lathe turnings and the cutting and fitting of the mortises and tenons are the results of many years of experience.

The wooden wheelbarrow wheel is composed of a central hub with radiating spokes fitting into curved pieces of wood known as felloes, which together make up the rim, over which a metal tire may or may not be fitted. The wheel is fitted onto an axle through a hole bored in the hub.

This type of wheel is simply constructed compared to the larger wagon wheels. Because of the difference in weight-carrying loads, the spokes of the wheelbarrow wheel do not have to be set into the hub on an angle as they are in the more dish-shaped wagon wheel.

Arthur Ernst cuts his hubs from well-seasoned maple or oak, both hardwoods with a fine grain and ones which will not split too easily. After turning the hub on the lathe, the positions of the mortises, into which the spokes will fit, must be calculated by measuring around the hub and then drawing the actual size of the spoke tenons on the hub.

There are always two spokes for each felloe, and they are made from ash which is split, not sawn, along the grain of the wood to make them as strong as possible. The spokes are smoothed down with a drawknife and a spokeshave making the end near the hub, the shoulder, larger than the end near the rim, the knock. A tenon is cut on the foot of the spoke to fit the mortise in the hub. The hub is clamped down on the workbench and the spokes are driven in with a heavy mallet. The outer ends of each spoke are then narrowed down into a round tongue, which will fit into holes bored through the felloes.

The curved felloes are not bent, they are cut. Their lines are carefully marked on a piece of ash using a compass and pencil, with the curves being at right angles to the grain of the wood. The felloes are fitted over the spoke-tongues and held in place with short wooden dowels driven into holes bored into the end of each felloe.

When this is complete, a rim is put on the wheel, usually by a blacksmith. Sometimes, both trades are practised by the same man, but like a great many other wheelwrights, Arthur Ernst sends his wheels to a neighbouring blacksmith for their metal tires.

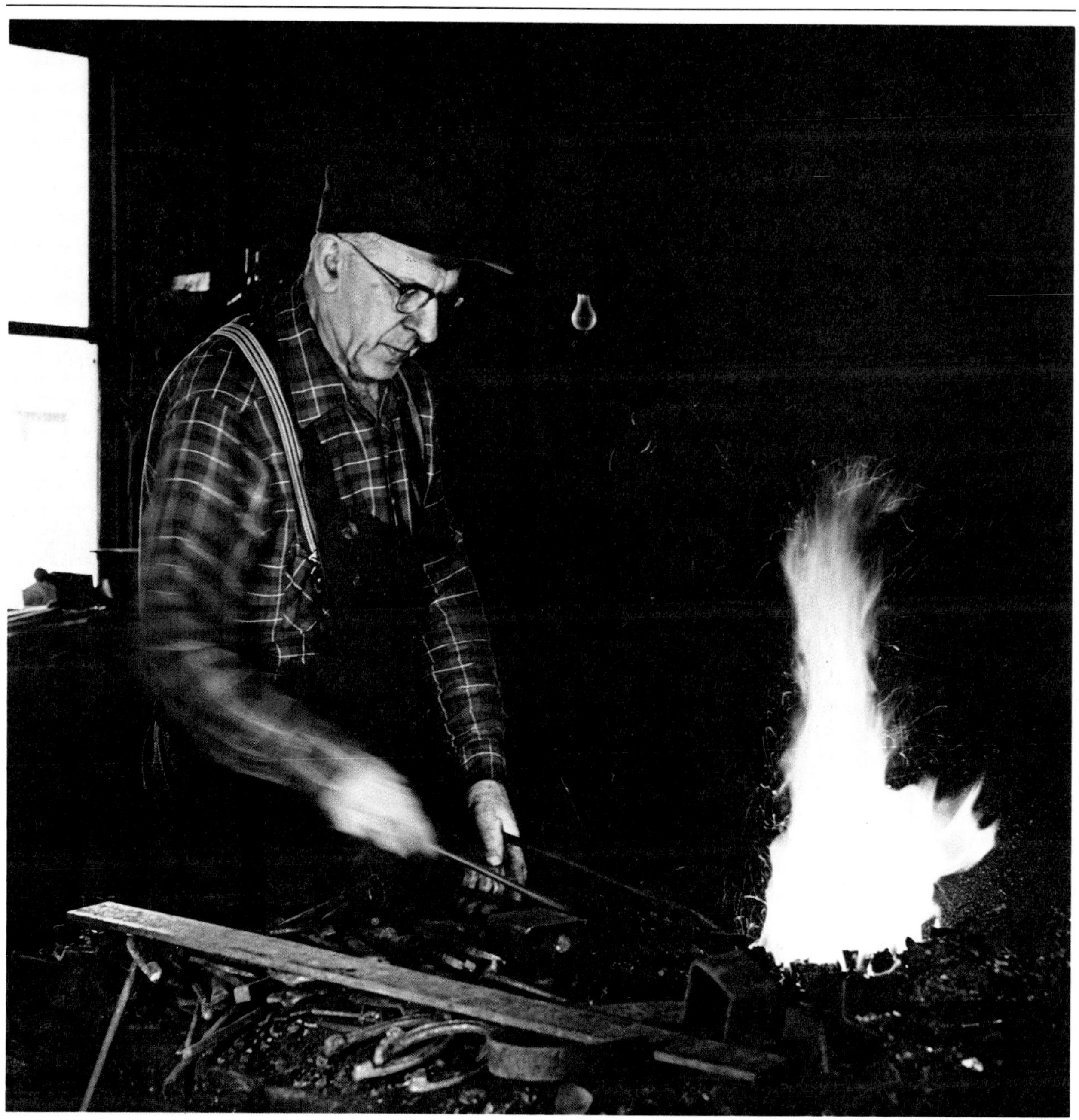

Archie McKnight

Born 15 May 1903, Blacksmith

I learnt my trade in Lyons Brook in Pictou County. My brother was a blacksmith – he was older than I was an' I went down there an' he wanted some help an' I started in with him – apprentice. That was in 1922. An' when I was learnin' my trade, you had to hold up your end an' take pride in it. But today, why, they don't take pride in much of anythin'. The most of 'em just work for their day's pay an' that's it.

Anyways, I knew a few fellers that used to come down here to Milton an' I thought I'd come down for a couple o' weeks an' see the country. I asked a feller here, I said, "Do you suppose I could make a livin' here?"

He said, "You'll get all the work you can do." I often think about him. That was 1928 an' I'm still here! The only blacksmith left in Queens County. Years ago, there was blacksmiths every four or five miles apart. Every little village had a blacksmith. In them days we made the wagons . . . what they call the Dutch wagon. It was all handmade. Outside of the hubs being turned out on a lathe. I made the whole thing. An' there was a lot of repair work too.

A lot o' people tell me, "What's goin' to happen when you can't do this?"

An' I say, "Well, I don't know." I've got two sons – no interest in blacksmithin' a'tall. The youngest is drivin' a truck. The oldest – he worked down in the garage for two or three months. An Air Force feller come down lookin' for recruits, an' he was layin' down underneath a truck in the winter – in the snow – an' he was layin' down underneath there puttin' a spring in. Snow an' the water was runnin' down in his face . . . he climbed out from underneath that

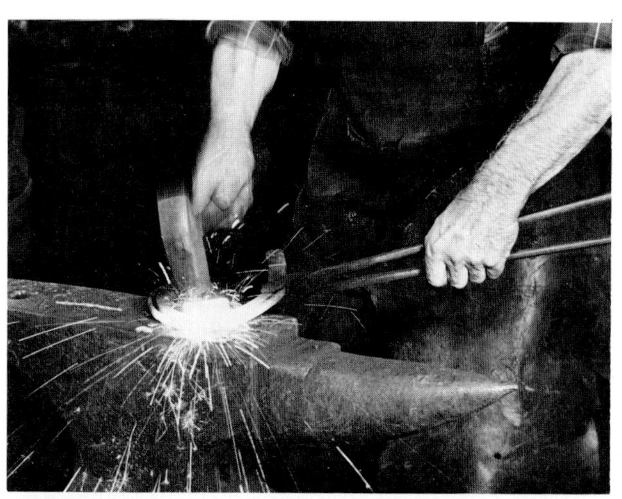

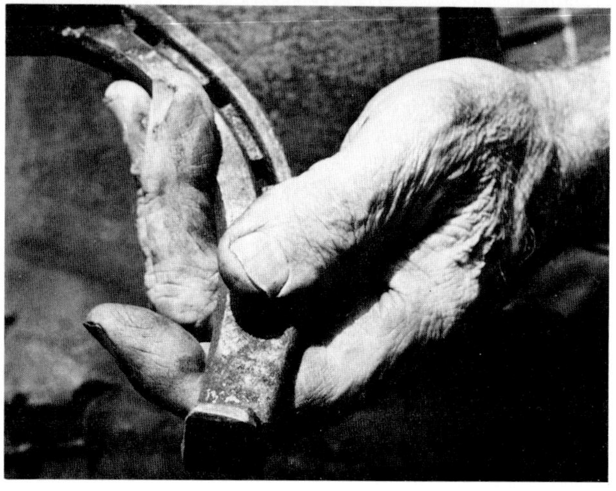

truck an' went up an' signed on. Oh my!

Yes, there's some change in my time. I tell you it's different today. Somethin' I often think about . . . the people today, they don't have time to stop an' talk to you. Now in them days you had a horse an' wagon. An' when you drove by, why if you was anywheres near a feller, you'd stop an' talk to him. An' why today the cars is goin' by . . . I don't know. The people aren't as happy an' contented today . . . always lookin' for somethin' they can't get, it seems to me. We're living' in a different world altogether.

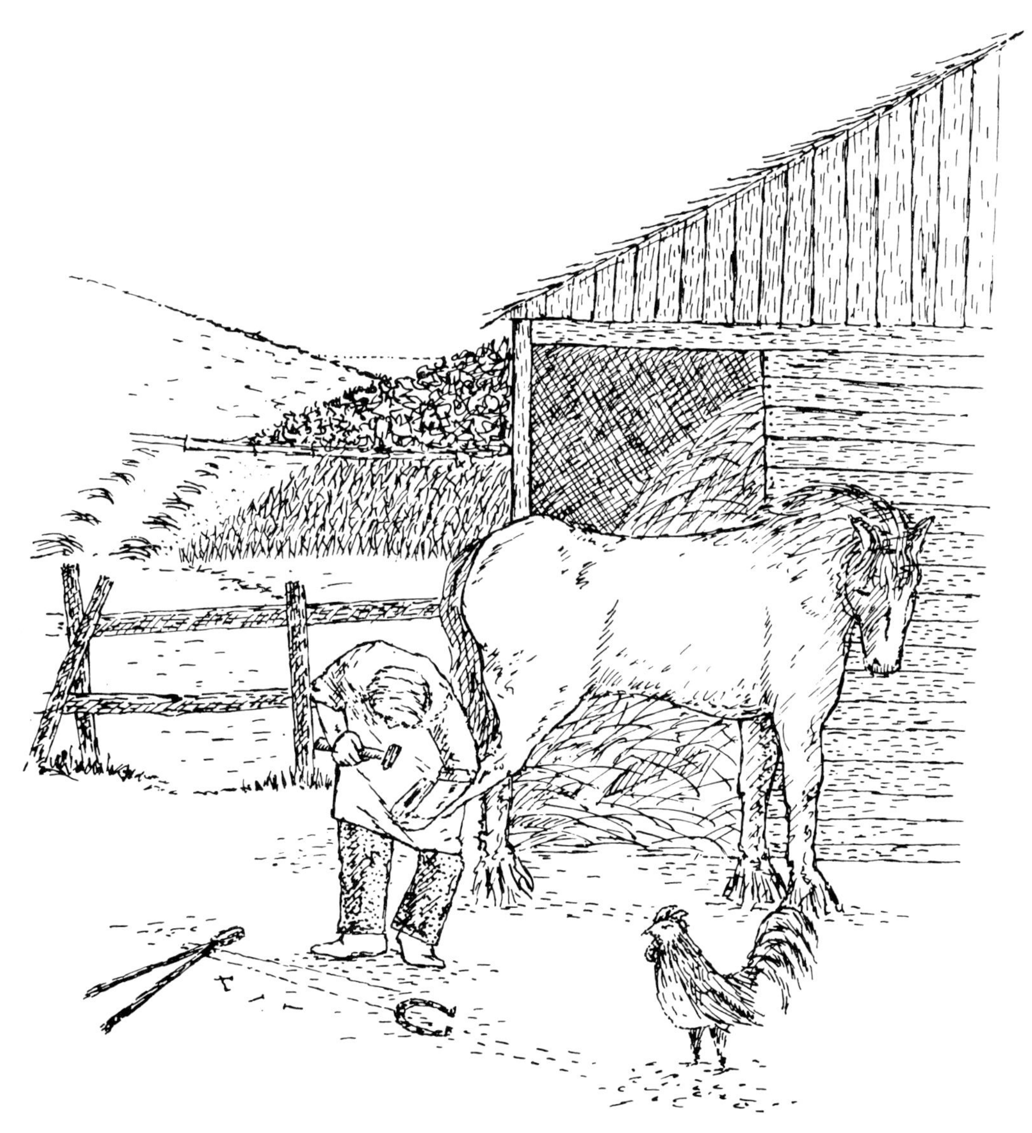

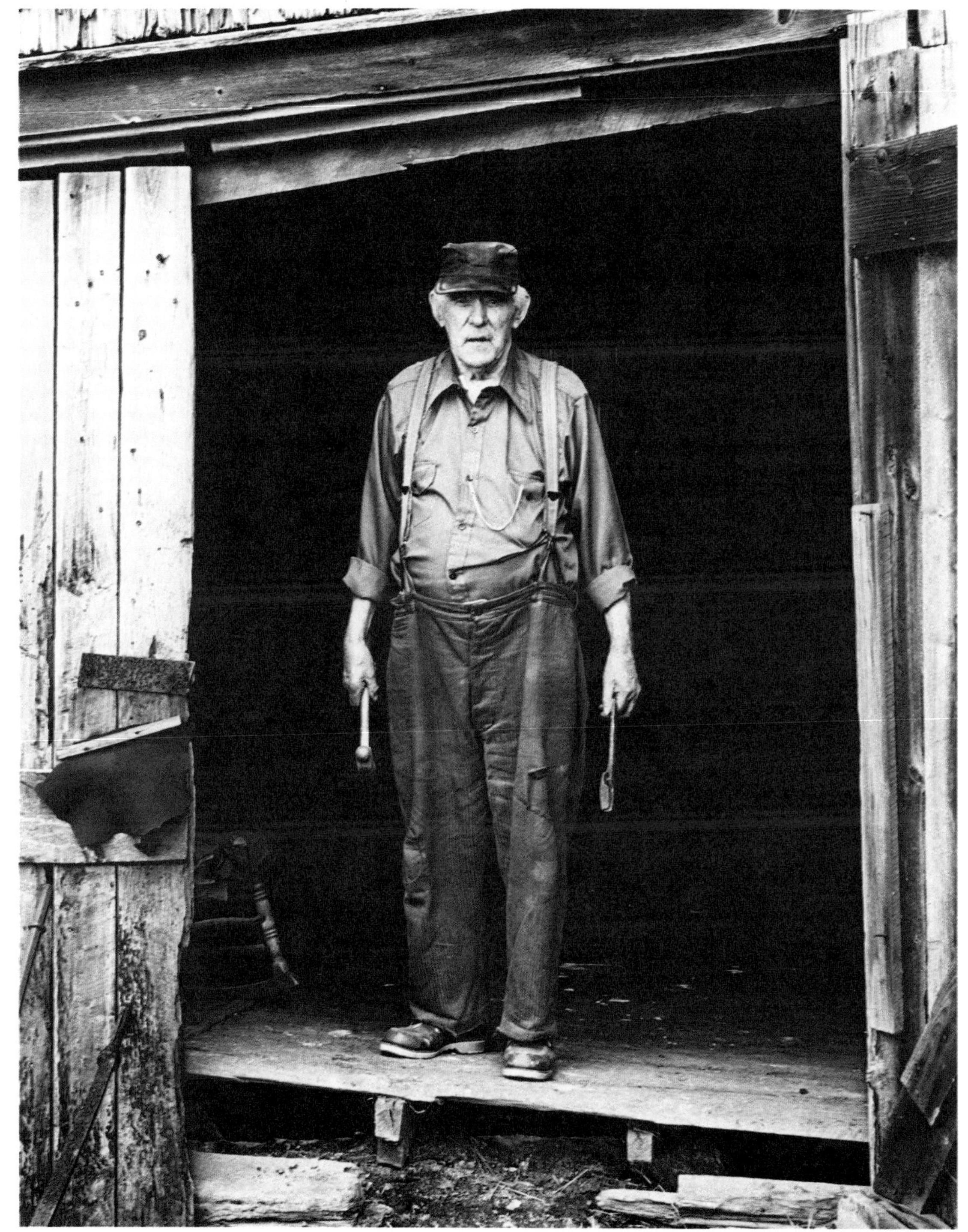

Freeland Minard

Born 20 May 1884, Blacksmith

On September the third, nineteen and three, I started as an apprentice with the old boss – that'd be Henry Bell. I got paid twenty-five dollars the first year, thirty dollars the second year, thirty-five dollars the third year, forty dollars the fourth year. An' in the first week of your fourth year – there were two forges in the shop – you was given a hammer an' a pair o' tongs, an' you was sent over to what we knew as the small fire. An' you had to go to work an' make a set o' tools to work with. You had to make your cold chisel or two and . . . two or three punches, different sizes, you see, and a pair o' tongs. . . . If you couldn't do it then, at the beginning of your fourth year, then you couldn't do it anywhere. That was your test.

Well then, as time went along, I took a new boy . . . an' taught him to strike. Striking in a blacksmith shop is . . . is quite an art. It's somethin' to learn – it takes three years to learn it . . . to strike fair. If the boss puts a punch down for you to punch on, you must strike that fair with your sledge. If you don't, you get a call down right away, you see. That's the reason the older boy takes the younger feller. At the end of four years I could go out an' take charge of a shop anywhere a'tall where there was the same kind o' work done. I spent four years to the last day at six o'clock with Mr. Bell. An' I remember . . . when he owed me . . . an' after supper when he . . . he owed me ten dollars. He paid me the ten dollars . . . an' he offered me another ten dollars, an' I wasn't goin' to take it. He said, "I want you to take it. That's for your good behaviour while you been here." So I had ten dollars . . . as a present. That was a lot in them days.

I'm ninety-three . . . I don't do

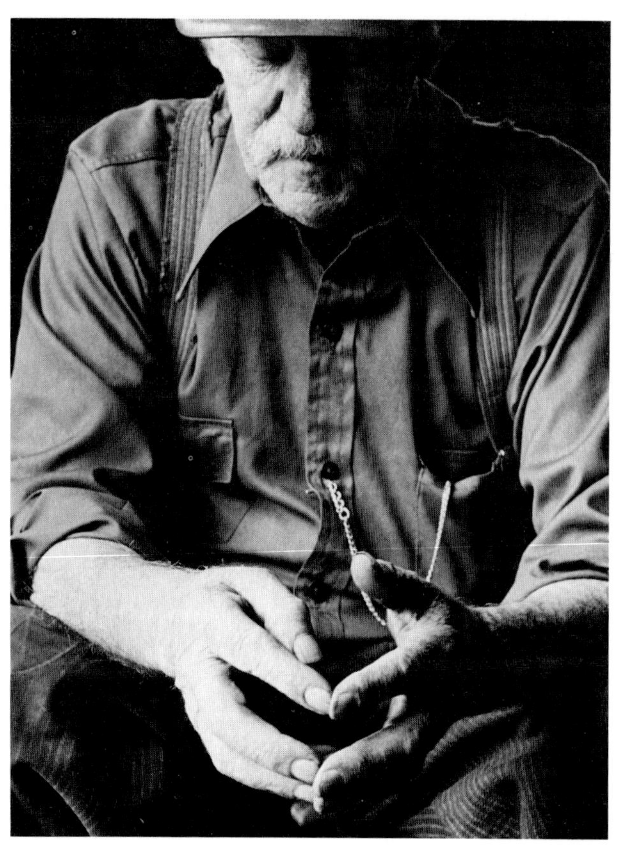

much blacksmithin' now. . . the odd job, but I'm just not . . . I walk down to the shop. I go down in the mornin' an' sit in the chair for quite a while. Some o' the fellers drop in to talk. It's half a mile. If I go down in the mornin' . . . an' go around for dinner, it's two miles. Exercise does me good.

Both Archie McKnight and Freeland Minard learned their trades during an apprenticeship with a practising blacksmith.

Until very recently, there were several blacksmiths working in every community in Nova Scotia making things ranging from farm tools to metal-tired wagon wheels. They sharpened knives and saws and shoed oxen, ponies and horses.

As Freeland Minard explains, they used to do certain chores at certain times of the year: "Take makin' ox shoes, in the summer or early fall, you might pile up a set of shoes–that's sixteen. Them shoes must be all one length, all one width, you see. You can't have one that long, and another one that long–you can't have that a'tall. Well then, as winter came on, we would steel caulk all of our ox shoes." Being resourceful, he used old gang-saws for the caulks, cutting the toe-caulk a little wider than the one for the heel, sprinkling it with borax and welding it to the steel shoes. Not all blacksmiths caulk in this way, some bend up each end of the shoe, but Freeland maintains his method makes a better shoe.

When Archie McKnight moved from Lyons Brook to Milton in 1930, the blacksmith shop there worked mostly with wagons, the "Dutch Wagon," and bobsleds. Most of the work was done by hand: ". . . outside of the hubs, I built the whole thing. An' there was a lot of repair work. When the tires wore out, we had to take the tires off, an' put new ones on. An' when the tires got loose, why we took 'em off, an' tighten 'em, you know, cut a little piece out an' weld 'em together again. To put 'em back on, we took 'em outside to the fire. We used to peel hemlock bark, an' that bark would make the fire hot an' we'd heat that tire, which was about five-eighths of an an inch smaller than the wheel–it would expand that much by heatin' in that hemlock fire. We'd carry the hot tire with big tongs over to wheel an' put it in place. Then, we would cool it off in a big tub of water. Sometimes, we'd pin the wheel, an' sometimes that rim'd tighten up enough not to use pins."

Archie has also made a good many claw-hoes in his day. This tool, looking much like a horseshoe attached to a short pole, has been used by gardeners in South Shore communities for generations–many maintain there is nothing better for digging up potatoes.

Although the number of blacksmiths in the province is declining, those who are working are kept busy. The shops are still gathering places for men to exchange the latest news and to reminisce in the warm glow of the forge.

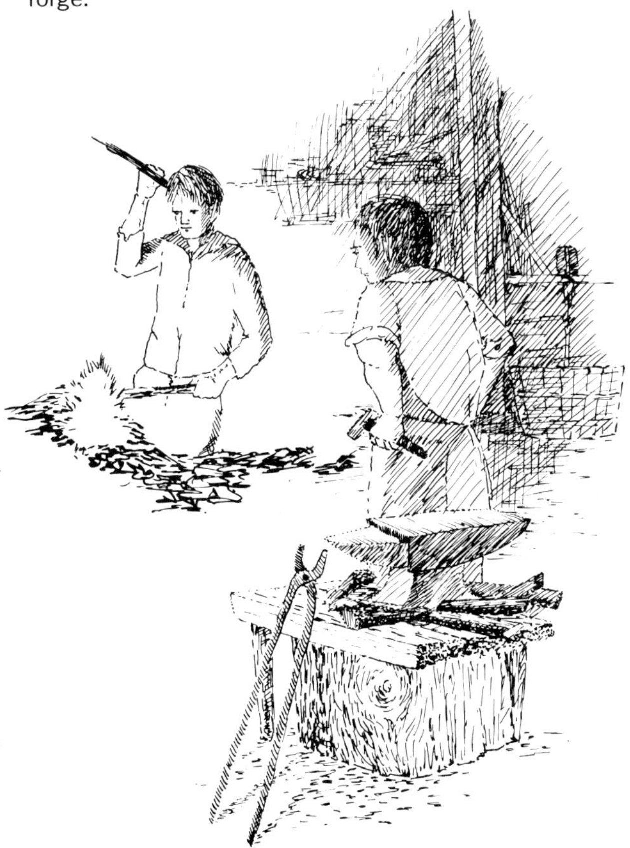

Bibliography

Adney, Edwin Tappan, and Howard I. Chapelle. *The Bark Canoes and Skin Boats of North America*. Bulletin 230. Washington, D. C.: Smithsonian Institution, 1964.

Ashley, Clifford W. *The Ashley Book of Knots*. New York: Doubleday & Co., 1944.

Barber, Joel. *Wild Fowl Decoys*. New York: Windward House, 1934.

Brasser, Ted J. *A Basketful of Indian Cultural Change*. Mercury Series, Canadian Ethnology Service Paper 22. Ottawa: National Museum of Man, 1975.

Burnham, Harold B., and Dorothy K. Burnham. *Keep Me Warm One Night: Early Handweaving in Eastern Canada*. Toronto: University of Toronto Press, 1972.

Clark, Andrew Hill. *Acadia: The Geography of Early Nova Scotia to 1760*. Madison, Wisconsin: University of Wisconsin Press, 1968.

Conroy, Mary. *Three Hundred Years of Canada's Quilts*. Toronto: Griffin House, 1976.

Creighton, Helen. *Folklore of Lunenburg County, Nova Scotia*. Toronto: McGraw-Hill Ryerson, 1976.

Davis, Marlene, et al. *A Nova Scotia Workbasket: Some Needlework Patterns Traditionally Used in the Province*. Halifax: Nova Scotia Museum, 1976.

de Kerchov, René. *International Maritime Dictionary*. New York: Van Nostrand Reinhold, 1948.

Douville, Raymond, and Jacques-Donat Casanova. *Daily Life in Early Canada from Champlain to Montcalm*. New York: Macmillan, 1968.

Eaton, Allen H. *Handicrafts of the Southern Highlands*. 1937; rpt. New York: Dover Publications, 1973.

Edlin, Herbert L. *Woodland Crafts of Britain: An Account of the Traditional Uses of Trees and Timbers in the British Countryside*. Newton Abbot: David and Charles, 1949.

Gordon, Joleen. *Edith Clayton's Market Basket: A Heritage of Splintwood Basketry in Nova Scotia*. Halifax: Nova Scotia Museum, 1977.

———. *Handwoven Hats: A History of Straw, Wood and Rush Hats in Nova Scotia*. Halifax: Nova Scotia Museum, 1980.

Hattinger, Franz. *The Duc de Berry's Book of Hours*. Berne, Switzerland: Hallwag, 1962.

Horwitz, Elinor L. *Mountain People, Mountain Crafts*. Philadelphia: J. B. Lippincott Company, 1974.

Jenkins, J. Geraint. *Traditional Country Craftsmen*. London: Routledge and Kegan Paul, 1965.

LeClercq, Chrestien. *New Relation of Gaspesia, with the Customs and Religion of the Gaspesian Indians*. 1691; rpt. Toronto: The Champlain Society, 1910.

McKendry, Ruth. *Quilts and Other Bed Coverings in the Canadian Tradition*. Toronto: Van Nostrand Reinhold, 1979.

Mackley, M. Florence. *Handweaving in Cape Breton*. Sydney, Nova Scotia: privately printed, 1967.

Manley, Atwood. *Rushton and His Times in American Canoeing*. Syracuse, New York: Syracuse University Press, 1968.

Martin, J. Lynton. *The Ross Farm Story*. Halifax: Nova Scotia Museum, 1974.

Mason, Otis Tufton. *Aboriginal Indian Basketry: Studies in a Textile Art without Machinery*. 1902; rpt. Glorieta, New Mexico: Rio Grande Press, 1972.

Meister, Rev. T. A. *The Apple Barrel Industry in Nova Scotia*. Halifax: Nova Scotia Museum, 1973.

Norwood, John. *Craftsmen at Work*. London: John Baker, 1977.

Osgood, William, and Leslie Hurley. *The Snowshoe Book*. Brattleboro, Vermont: Stephen Green Press, 1975.

Rand, Silas Tertius. *Dictionary of the Language of the Micmac Indians who Reside in Nova Scotia, New Brunswick.* Halifax: Nova Scotia Printing Co., 1888.

Saunders, Mary. *A Nova Scotia Workbasket*.

Shaw, Barbara. *The Village Blacksmith*. Halifax: Nova Scotia Museum, 1972.

Sloane, Eric. *A Museum of Early American Tools*. New York: Ballantine Books, 1964.

Sparling, Mary. *A Guide to Some Domestic Pioneer Skills*. Halifax: Nova Scotia Museum, 1972.

Stephens, David. *Forgotten Trades of Nova Scotia*. Halifax: Petheric Press, 1972.

Summerhays, R. S. *Summerhays' Encyclopaedia for Horsemen*. London: Frederick Warne and Co., 1970.

Tunis, Edwin. *Colonial Craftsmen and the Beginnings of American Industry*. New York: World Publishing, 1972.

"A Visit with Jack Sam Hinkley." *Cape Breton Magazine*. Number 16 (June 1977), pp. 1-5.

Whitehead, Ruth. *Elitekey: Micmac Material Culture from 1600 to the Present*. Halifax: Nova Scotia Museum, 1980.

About the Authors

Peter Barss traces his Nova Scotian ancestry back to Captain Joseph Barss of Lunenburg County, master of a notorious privateer called the Liverpool Packet. He lives in West Dublin on the South Shore of Nova Scotia with his wife and two sons.

Barss studied photography at the School of the Boston Museum of Fine Arts. After an early career as a teacher, he decided to devote his full time to photography. His photographs have been published in numerous magazines, have been purchased by the National Film Board of Canada and the Nova Scotia Art Bank, and have been chosen for group shows in Canada and the United States. He is an artist whose work reflects painstaking care and a deep respect for the Nova Scotian heritage of his subjects.

Two exhibits of Barss's work are currently being circulated across Canada by the Nova Scotia Museum as part of the National Museums programme. *Images of Lunenburg County*, the first collection, was published in book form in 1978. The second collection, *Older Ways: Traditional Nova Scotian Craftsmen* appears in this book.

Joleen Gordon wrote the notes on traditional crafts for *Older Ways*. After working as a marine biologist, she has spent the past eight years studying traditional crafts. She is a Research Associate with the Nova Scotia Museum in Halifax and a consultant in traditional Nova Scotian crafts for the Massey Foundation Craft Collection. Her work on handcrafts has been published by the Nova Scotia Museum, *Canadian Geographic* and other magazines. Gordon lives in Dartmouth with her husband and two daughters.

Designed by Hugh Michaelson
Typeset by Alpha Graphics Limited in Goudy Old Style with craft notes in Trade Gothic and display lines in Columbus
Printed by The Bryant Press Limited on Warren's Patina Matte
Bound by The Bryant Press Limited in case material by Columbia Mills